D0394255

A National Conversation Continues

"Ken Dryden's *Becoming Canada* is a timely, passionate, urgent, and provocative book that dares parliamentarians and citizens to re-imagine our politics and our future as a country. It launches an important debate about what Canada could and should be."   — *Guy Vanderhaeghe*

"Ken Dryden is obsessed with finding the story of Canada, a narrative we can believe in and which — in his words — will make us better. *Becoming Canada* is a personal and deeply committed work of national storytelling written from an exceptionally valuable point of view. Full of detail, care and passion, this is a book that speaks of who we are, and who we must aspire to become."   — *Atom Egoyan*

"Ken Dryden and I don't agree on how new Canadians need to fit in. But we do agree on how great a country this is and how we need to know that about ourselves. And what he writes about politics is fantastic. Read this book."
                                                  — *Don Cherry*

"Some guys, you ask them the time and they build you a watch.

In Dryden's head is a big country 'hidden by politics,' a country trying, busting to get out from behind tall shadows and the time is required.

For the young and the old, this is the kinda book we've been waiting for.

And, really, isn't it time? For a guy who will lay it all out there?

Simply, like a teacher? How it is, how it could be, open, brave free, that we're more than 'this politics,' that friendship changes your life?"   — *Gord Downie*

Join the conversation at becomingcanada.ca

BECOMING CANADA

ALSO BY KEN DRYDEN

The Game

Home Game: Hockey and Life in Canada (with Roy MacGregor)

The Moved and the Shaken: The Story of One Man's Life

In School: Our Kids, Our Teachers, Our Classrooms

KEN DRYDEN

BECOMING CANADA

MᶜCLELLAND & STEWART

Library and Archives Canada Cataloguing in Publication

Dryden, Ken, 1947-
Becoming Canada : our story, our politics, our future / Ken Dryden.

ISBN 978-0-7710-2945-5

1. Canada – Politics and government – 2006-. 2. Canada – History – 21st century.
3. Canada. 4. National characteristics, Canadian. I. Title.

FC640.D97 2010   971.07'3   C2010-905156-4

We acknowledge the financial support of the Government of Canada through the
Book Publishing Industry Development Program and that of the Government of
Ontario through the Ontario Media Development Corporation's Ontario Book
Initiative. We further acknowledge the support of the Canada Council for the
Arts and the Ontario Arts Council for our publishing program.

Typeset in Van Dijck by M&S, Toronto
Printed and bound in Canada

ANCIENT FOREST
FRIENDLY

This book is printed on acid-free paper that is
100% ancient-forest friendly (100% post-consumer waste).

McClelland & Stewart Ltd.
75 Sherbourne Street
Toronto, Ontario
M5A 2P9
www.mcclelland.com

1 2 3 4 5   14 13 12 11 10

To our ancestors who have written us this story;
to our children who are writing it anew.

THE CAUTIONARY TALE is important both to literature and public discourse. *Brave New World, Nineteen Eighty-Four, Fahrenheit 451, The Handmaid's Tale*—all have taken a certain human experience and pushed it, implication by implication, into a future that is credible, recognizable, and frightening. In doing so, the cautionary tale aims to create a sufficient dramatic awareness that will in turn generate an action.

In today's world, which seems to be powering on toward disastrous climate change and unrelenting conflict no matter what our governments do, what's more important than awareness is the belief that something *can* be done and the ability to see *how* it can be done. Without belief and ability, we are unable to muster the necessary will to tackle the big questions. Today, more important than seeing what is wrong is *imagining* how we can correct it. More important than the cautionary tale is the aspirational tale.

PREFACE

As I WAS FINISHING writing this book, I read an article in the *New York Times* by David Segal headlined "IT'S COMPLICATED." Segal wrote about the overwhelmingly complex problems of the time—the Afghanistan and Iraq wars, the recession, health care, and probably what triggered the piece: the giant oil spill in the Gulf of Mexico. Segal cited an anthropologist at the University of Utah, Joseph Tainter, author of *The Collapse of Complex Societies*, who in his examination of three ancient civilizations concluded that bankruptcy caused by complexity brought about their collapse. "'Everything the Roman emperors did was a reasonable response in the situation they found themselves in,'" Tainter said in an interview with Segal. "'It was the cumulative impact that did them in.'"

Segal also cited Brenda Zimmerman, a professor at York University's Schulich School of Business, who suggested that in dealing with large problems, one must cut through the complexity to the simple principles at the core of any issue. In concluding the article, Segal returned to his original premise: "[C]omplexity has a way of defeating good intentions. As we clean up these messes, there is no point in hoping for a new age of simplicity. The best we can do is hope the solutions are just complicated enough to work."

I thought, How wrong Segal is. Yes, we do have far more information today than we have ever had. We have microscopes that probe deeper and telescopes that search farther; we have processes that analyze information to create new information, to create new ways of looking at things, which in turn generate even more new information. Everything from a simple widget to an earthworm can be made to seem complex. But behind this noise of complexity, the essential issue is what *really* matters. Complexity didn't cause the collapse of those ancient civilizations. If complexity played a role, it was because those societies had lost the common understanding of themselves that had allowed them to distinguish between what mattered and what didn't matter. They had lost their common story, a story which had given them a reason not only to say "yes" but also to say "no" to any new idea or direction. As a result, as Tainter said, the "cumulative impact" of obligations overburdened and overwhelmed them.

Failure seems complicated. Success usually doesn't. The challenge is to find an understanding that can help make the complicated more explicable and to allow for choices to be made. It is why stories matter so much— they help us connect with one another. They embody common experiences that remind us, as people and as countries, of all we share. Without these stories, we search out and fixate on differences. If we don't matter together as many, we make ourselves matter apart one from another, insisting on a distinct identity of our own. It is important to respect complexity, but it is critical to find in complexity the simplicity that holds us together as people, as countries, and as a world.

In this book, I look at what happens when we, as individuals or countries, have the wrong story about ourselves, or when we have lost our story, and when we need a new one. There are references to the mire and challenge of politics, and to the possibilities of politics. We see the consequences of story and politics uniting— and clashing. For some Canadians, this experience may be most vividly seen outside Canada, as I illustrate in my discussion of "America" and Obama, of Copenhagen and climate change; for others, this is embodied in Stephen Harper and Michael Ignatieff, the Conservative

Party and the Liberal Party. My chapters on Ottawa and politics suggest that story has been left behind—politics is so absorbing to political insiders, politicians, and the political media that it makes you forget story. That is the test politics presents. But in this book, one story recurs. One story challenges and haunts politics. This book isn't about politics, Obama, Harper, or Ignatieff, or about stories in general. This book is about Canada.

In many ways, I have been writing this book all my life. And so I want to thank the people who have made and shared my life. My parents, Murray and Margaret Dryden; my grandmother Ethel Campbell, who lived with us through my childhood; my brother, Dave, and sister, Judy, and their families; my wife's parents, Richard and Evelyn Curran; her sisters and brother and their families; my classmates and teachers, teammates and coaches in the Toronto suburb of Etobicoke; the people of Montreal and Quebec, my teammates, coaches, and friends; the people in cities and tiny towns everywhere in the country who have allowed me into their lives and sometimes into their homes, who have put up with my questions, and who have been willing to think about and share their feelings about themselves, their communities, and their country. They have been my teachers and my fellow-learners. They have given me, and continue to give me, a lifetime of energy and inspiration.

I want to thank those who have given me a chance—co-workers, hockey people, government people, publishers—who have been willing to see in me something beyond the obvious—jock, goalie, student, lawyer, politician—and who have allowed me and encouraged me always to try and to do.

I want to thank those who have shared my life in politics for the last six years. People in riding associations who believe in their party, whatever party, and others who are not members of any party but who believe that their government and their Canada matter. People I agree with, and people I do not, but people who want life to be better, who hope and believe it can be better. People who have challenged me and who have made me think more deeply and feel more intensely.

I want to thank those who have helped me in the writing of this book. David Staines, my editor, who saw this as a book and believed in it before I did and who has believed in it every step of the way. Jenny Bradshaw and Heather Sangster, who shared my ambitions and offered their professionalism. Cory Pike and Linda Kristal, who read various drafts and offered their smart perspectives and advice. Chris Hall, Terry O'Malley, and Kevin Sugden, who have taught me different ways to tell stories. A wish list of authors, artists, and others I put together, some of whom I knew, some I didn't, who were willing to read a speech I had given at universities and to talk about Canada, at length and fully engaged, and who offered me what I most needed as I was still feeling my way, their enthusiasm.

I want to thank our kids, Sarah Dryden-Peterson and Michael Dryden, their spouses, and their kids. They have allowed my wife and me to see the world again through their eyes. Once, they learned through us; now we learn through them. And most particularly, I want to thank my wife, Lynda Dryden. Lynda is my first editor and my last editor. She has the toughest job. She knows my hope, and she sees what she sees on the page. She has somehow been able to keep me more "up" than I have earned and less "down" than I deserve, but not too "up" for the real work ahead. She gives me confidence.

Ottawa
June 2010

PROLOGUE

I GREW UP IN A FAMILY who expected three things: that we try hard, do the best that is in us to do, and be fair. My parents expected no different from my older brother, my younger sister, or me than they did from themselves. They didn't expect that we would be geniuses as students, superstars as athletes or artists, or millionaires. But they did expect us to aspire to something. Life was exciting. There were important things to do—for a family, for a community, for a country. If we were good enough, we didn't have the right *not* to be good enough.

We had been given a lot—a healthy body and mind, a nurturing home, a safe community to grow up in, and parents who loved us. My parents expected us to take ourselves seriously. To them, there was no such thing as "only" anything—"only" a game, "only" a test, not an exam. If something was important enough to do, it was important enough to do it well.

Yet my parents were never grim or heavy-handed in their messages. All this was simply obvious to them and, over time, to us too. When my friends were allowed to do things I wasn't, I would argue with my father: "They can do it, why can't I?" knowing that I had the better argument. Each time his answer was the same: "You don't want to be like everyone else, do you?" That was as lecture-like as our encounters were. My parents made things fun. They gave us opportunities to have different experiences, to visit different places, to love what we were doing. They made a bigger point of "try" than they did of "success." Success was ultimately out of our hands; try was not. They were in life for the long run, for our long run, and they expected the same from us. And as long as we tried, they believed, we should dream because who knows what's in us unless we do.

About "nature," after the moment of our conception, my parents couldn't do anything; about "nurture," they could. Although I was good at a number of things, my family made me better. My parents knew what everyone at the time knew: family expectations mattered.

I played on a hockey team, the Montreal Canadiens, who expected us to win each and every game in each and every year, and to win in a special way. We had an owner who, in the sometimes internal tension between money and winning, never compromised us. We had a general manager who found the best players to build a team. We had a coach who was able to teach, push, prod, inspire, and motivate to get the best from us. We had teammates who made us skate faster, play smarter, and compete harder because they did. We had the best arena to play in and fans who would never let us forget that what we were doing mattered. The team gave us every chance to be the best, to feel satisfaction fully, to feel pride fully. The team put *our* destiny into our own hands. If we didn't win, we knew it was our fault. I was good, but the right team made me better.

The team did all this because the Canadiens knew they were special. Howie Morenz and Georges Vézina, Rocket Richard and Jean Béliveau, Doug Harvey and Jacques Plante had triumphed. What right had we not to triumph ourselves? When people asked why the Canadiens won so often, the answer was always the same: "It's the Canadiens tradition," commentators said, and everyone nodded. They knew what everyone at the time knew: tradition mattered.

My post-hockey life began during a period when companies were being analyzed more and more to determine why some succeeded and others didn't. What was different about each of them, in their values and attitudes, in how they understood themselves, in the way they did things large and small? People came to talk not about a company's expectations or traditions but about its "culture." Some companies had the right culture, some didn't. And those that had the right culture made a good employee better.

Later, I worked as the Ontario Youth Commissioner with disadvantaged youth who grew up without constructive family expectations, traditions, or personal culture. Most of these young people had dropped out of school; all were unemployed. Where had life gone wrong for them? They needed something else in their lives to help make them better.

I wrote a book, *The Moved and the Shaken*, about "an average guy." Non-fiction books are almost always written about someone the public deems as special in some important way—prime ministers or presidents, generals, rock stars, athletes, CEOs, even crooks. I wanted to write about someone unknown to anyone except their own family and friends, neighbours and co-workers; someone who was around forty, married with at least one child, lived in a suburb, had a high school education, earned an average income from an average job. Someone who, as others who knew him would say, was an average guy. What made him what he was? And what, in his "nature" and his "nurture," might have made his life better?

In writing my next book, *In School*, about education, I decided to go back to high school for a year. I sat in class every day to see who excelled as a student and who didn't, and to try to understand why. Why does one student get a 90 in math, another a 58? What is it in these students' lives that makes this difference? What might make a difference now? In my observation of these students, the words *family expectations* did not capture the essential point, nor did personal *tradition* or *culture*. Some kids had the proper understanding about themselves, and some didn't. Those who didn't walked into math class every day, their heads filled with "I hate math. I can't do math. I'm never going to be a scientist or an engineer. Why do I have to take this? Why am I here?" For the math teacher, a good lesson plan and a cheery disposition weren't going to make a sufficient difference. These students had the wrong "story" about themselves. If anything was going to change, that teacher would have to help the students write a different story.

I also worked for the Toronto Maple Leafs, whose story had once been much like that of the Montreal Canadiens. Then it changed, becoming one of greed and perpetual disappointment, where out of the internal tension between money and winning, making money mattered a little more than winning. People liked to say that because the Leafs didn't *need* to win, they didn't win. Whether this story was true, and over time it has become less true, it had the power of being true. No matter what the Leafs did, something would happen; they couldn't manage to win. The explanation was not "It's the Leafs tradition"; it was "Same old Leafs." Many of the Leafs players were good. The right team, a team with the right story, would have made them better.

Now I am a Member of Parliament. It is my job both to represent one riding, York Centre, in old suburban Toronto, and to represent Canada. I was born in Hamilton; I grew up in the Toronto suburb of Etobicoke. I spent four years in Ithaca, New York, while I attended Cornell University. I lived a year in Winnipeg, eight years in Montreal, a year in Ottawa, another year in Cambridge, England, and now twenty-nine years in Toronto, the last six years living much of the time in Ottawa as an MP. I have been to every province and every territory—and almost every part of every province and territory—many times. It is the privilege that comes with being a former hockey player and now MP; it is also the privilege that comes from growing up in a family who wanted always to "see for themselves." The privilege is not in being in airports, hotels, or banquet halls; it is not in the comings and goings. The real privilege is in hanging around an extra day or two, talking to people about their lives, their families, their jobs, their towns, their Canada, their hopes and fears and dreams.

The Canada I see has never been the Canada I have read about and heard about. Of course, I do see the winter—I played in it!—I see the mountains and lakes and wide-open spaces. I see the bigness and the smallness of Canada. I see the challenge to exist, to survive, to be Canada. And I see the United States everywhere. Growing up in Toronto in the 1950s, we received three television stations, two of which were from Buffalo, and except for *Hockey Night in Canada* and *The Wayne & Shuster Hour*, all the good shows—*The Ed Sullivan Show*, *I Love Lucy*, *The Jackie Gleason Show*, *The Garry Moore Show*, *The Red Skelton Show*, *Bonanza*, the Saturday baseball *Game of the Week*—were on the Buffalo stations. But even then I didn't see Canada as an inconsequential place. I didn't see Canada as disappointing. I didn't see a place that seemed more what it was not—*not* the United States, *not* Britain, *not* France—than what it was. I didn't see a place where things always fell short. Yet in Canada we have always had an all-purpose justification that would spring from our mouths the moment failure happened, often before: "Typically Canadian, eh?" I never found the phrase as funny as others did. To

me, it was not true enough to be funny, and too embarrassing if it was true.

For many years I found the "Typically Canadian, eh?"
version of Canada annoying. Then it made me mad.
That phrase has the same effect as a teacher dismissing
yet another incorrect answer from a struggling but determined student—"Typical Jane." Or a hockey coach
saying to a player who could never quite score but
who had spent the previous summer analyzing, visual-
izing, and practising again and again only to hit the
goalpost on a breakaway on his first day of training
camp—"Typical Fred." For companies, for families,
for teams, and for countries too, such a phrase has the
same crippling effect that makes everything impossible and every future the same as every past.

For my first eighteen months in Ottawa, I was part of
Paul Martin's government as the minister of social development. It was a busy time. We were doing so much,
and there was so much we weren't doing. We weren't
doing many small tasks that, given the overwhelming
magnitude of what a government does, might escape
any administration. We also weren't doing much about
many large questions about which there was no political
dispute: too many people in the country living the way
no Canadian should have to live; economic competi-
tiveness in a rapidly changing global world; climate

change risking life on Earth. The problem wasn't that we were unaware. We seemed to be missing only the right policy, only the right program. We seemed to suffer only a lack of creativity and imagination. As soon as we found the right words, everything would be different. But that wasn't the problem. The problem was that we didn't think we could do more. This wasn't only a problem for the Liberals; this was a problem for parliamentarians of every party. The problem was how we saw ourselves.

We have paid a huge price for having the wrong sense of ourselves as a country. It has forced us to live under a ceiling of expectation and ambition that is so far below what we can do and can be. It is so far below our proper ceiling that anything governments or individuals can imagine themselves doing—economically, socially, environmentally, internationally—is too modest and too inconsequential. What we should do in the bigger world about climate change and hunger, and what we should do at home about poverty, depends on whether we see ourselves—wrongly—as relatively small and powerless, economically, culturally, and militarily a backwater far from where the action is; or whether we see ourselves as the Canada we are, today and now. As a person, as a company, as a team, or as a country, if you have the wrong story, you get the wrong answer.

I have come to believe after six years as an MP that the direction and ambition of Canada's policies, and the nature of our politics, will not change much no matter what party is in power if our understanding of ourselves as a country doesn't change. All this genial, ambition-killing self-deprecation is no longer simply annoying. If we don't conceive of our story of Canada accurately, we as politicians can't do what we need to do, and we as citizens can't live the life that is in us to live. If we don't get our story right, our politics will do what politics always does; it will turn everything into politics. We can see that now in the ups and downs of Obama. We can see that now in the global story of climate change and the international politics of Copenhagen. We can see that now in ourselves. But if we do get Canada's story right, if it is strong enough and proud enough, if it is deep enough inside our bones, that story will rise above— and exist above—politics. It will challenge politics; it will change politics.

We are good. A Canada with the right story will make us better.

"AMERICA"

BOOKSHELVES ARE FILLED with advice on how to change ourselves—our looks, weight, clothes, spouses, kids, pets—and on how we live, how we think, and how to do life again.

How does a country change itself? How does a world? If some big realities about a country or about the world change and if old, ineffective ways don't work any longer, what do we do then? To find an answer, for Canadians, it is instructive to look at the United States and Obama, and to the climate-change debate.

We live in a world where destruction is easy. Not just wholesale destruction by nuclear bombs, for example, but the killing of hundreds, if not thousands, by simple but deadly materials that cost almost nothing and can be put together in a basement or a shed. Where once this capacity for destruction had taken a country to afford its cost, to do its science, to deliver its blow, where once it had taken an army to unleash its devastating power, it now takes only one person who believes in something just as strongly as does a nation of a few hundred million and who feels his or her belief is no less worthy because he or she is only one person. This person may also believe that killing the right people in this life will lead to a better life for all eternity, while many of those he or she is fighting don't believe in a life after this life and need to squeeze every possible second out of this one. One person has everything to gain; another has everything to lose.

We live in a world where we can no longer get away from one another. There is no mountain or desert or ocean that can't be crossed; no wall built high enough, no fortress so fully defended, no political or economic boundary that can protect us. Information and viruses travel freely, as does envy and resentment. We can no longer isolate ourselves within our own language, culture, or religion. It is not possible to imagine transforming everyone else to make them just like us. No one is going to conquer the world. The only way is to listen, discuss, learn, respect, negotiate, compromise, work together. There is no way out but to get along.

We live in a world of nearly 7 billion people, a population that can sustain itself only as long as many millions die each year of malnutrition and many millions more of preventable diseases, as long as hundreds of millions have a life expectancy of less than fifty years, and as long as several billion don't insist on living, or don't have the capacity to live, a Western middle-class life.

What if the 2.5 billion people of China and India, twice the population of Europe and North America combined, were to have this capacity and insisted on living a Western lifestyle? Environmentally, we could not sustain the possibility—the planetary math doesn't work. Yet year after year, we see both China's and India's capacity grow, we see that insistence increase— there are now 10 million cars in China, up from fewer than 1 million just eight years ago—and we see that destruction escalate too.

We live on a planet that was not made for—or even made *especially* for—human beings. A mere shift of three degrees in the world's temperature—from 14°C to 17°C or -24°C to -21°C—a change not great enough to make us take off or put on a sweater—could melt glacier ice; alter evaporation and precipitation pat-terns; change ocean currents and atmospheric air flows; reduce available water for human consumption, agri-culture, and energy use; generate more violent hurri-canes and other extremes of weather and, in fact, more extremes of all kinds—floods, droughts, fires, diseases; and create deserts, destroy rain forests, and raise water levels. In short, this temperature shift would cause disruption, increase stress on people and structures, and generate more and more unknowns—turning a life we know how to live, even if it wasn't always desirable, into a life we don't know how to live. Only three degrees.

Human beings appeared on this planet only in the last 2.5 million years, which in Earth-time is hardly a blink ago. For almost all those years, we didn't matter much. We were only a few million in number. We weren't large or strong. We didn't dominate our landscape like a saber-toothed tiger, woolly mammoth, or bison did. We lived only a few years. We were only one of countless other species—like an otter or a parrot.

For all but the last few hundred years, our existence on Earth has been modest. Other living beings had greater muscular power—they were able to run faster and longer and overpower their prey—or had greater physical weapons—bigger teeth, stronger jaws, powerful claws. Others could see or hear or sense far better. Not long ago, we developed our own greater power—to think—and with that to create memory, learn, conceive of the future, work together, plan, and make tools to do work that had once been beyond our capacity. We developed this greater power sufficiently to allow us to live longer, do more, make more, have more—and also to cut down, build over, pollute, and kill off other species, bringing about their extinction. As human beings, we are able to live for our own convenience, to create weapons of mass destruction, to change our climate, to put life at risk.

How does a world change its story? How does a country? This is what U.S. president Barack Obama was talking about during his 2008 election campaign. He didn't ask the American people the question that all political challengers ask, "Are you better off now than you were four years ago?" He asked them, instead, to stop and look around at America itself: "Is *this* the real America we see?"

The war in Iraq? Torture? Health care that has no room for tens of millions of citizens? The exaggerated wealth and the exaggerated poverty and the exaggerated gap between them—is that what the United States stands for? Is this the American dream? Is the purpose of all this freedom and liberty only to accumulate more and more and more? More and bigger cars, more food, more *things*, more than Americans can use, more than they even care about, more than is good for them—as people, as a society, as a planet. This obesity of body, mind, and spirit that has crept into their lives and seems unstoppable. "Is this the real America we see?" Obama asked the American people. "No," he answered. "We are better than this."

More than being about economic prosperity, national security, the environment, or even justice or fairness, Obama's message during the campaign was about "America": "the land of the free and the home of the brave," "the land of opportunity," the "melting pot" for the world's peoples. "America": that special place of forever new frontiers—geographical, intellectual—of forever optimism, forever possibility, and forever becoming. The United States is a physical place; "America" is a place of the heart and of the imagination. "America," Obama was saying, is their best story and their right story. And what makes "America" special is not its separation of powers and checks and balances, it is not its separation of church and state, or even its frontier. What makes "America" special is its "specialness," that instinct and capacity always to do the important and necessary thing when it needs to be done. To reinvent itself, to be able and willing to go off in new, amazing directions, yet always to stay at the centre, still to be "America."

Because the world changes, what is important and necessary is not the same at every moment. What made the United States special during the twentieth century, in the last age of empire, was its overwhelming economic and military power. The United States used its abundant resources, more abundant than anyone else's, to make things the world would come to want. It made weapons that could win hot wars and cold wars. And because being bigger, richer, and more powerful had made the United States special, it seemed to most Americans that being bigger, richer, and more powerful was what special was. The United States kept on being that America in Vietnam, Kuwait, Iraq, and Afghanistan. It continued to be that America in creating SUVs and sub-prime mortgages. It kept on being that America even as the world community was shaking its head, wondering where "America" had gone. All this came to a disastrously clear focus with George W. Bush, who, with his blue jeans, Texas ranch, and love of baseball, was the most American yet least "American" of all presidents—in image, a Teddy Roosevelt but a century out of time. The world had changed; what defined "specialness" had changed; and what America needed to do to be "America" had changed. George W. Bush hadn't noticed.

Now we live in a global community in which no one country, not even the United States, is big enough or strong enough economically or militarily to control and dominate. In a global community, specialness is not the Iraq War or SUVs; specialness is being smart enough to see the ice caps melting and to know that the age of carbon is coming to a close. It is being smart enough to launch "America" into "the next thing," as if on a mission to the moon, to develop new benign energies, to restructure the economy, to change the way people live. It is being smart enough to change our relationship with the planet and with other nations and peoples, to get along with others, to get along with the planet, to get ahead and to stay ahead, yet to bring along others in the task.

And "America" is about succeeding. In "America," you don't just say something, you do it, and there is always a way. That is not optimism. That is not Obama's legendary hopefulness. That is "America," and that is Obama's own life experience of "America." "Yes, we can" is not so much a slogan as it is a simple observation. It was "America's" phrase long before it was ever Obama's because it had been America's experience played out thousands of times a day, year after year. Succeeding is not about ideology; it is going where your best answers are, wherever they are. And specialness is about feeling the pride and excitement that were once a part of being American. Specialness is doing the important and necessary thing when it needs to be done.

Americans are good, Obama was saying. They need only the right story; they need "America" to make them better.

The son of a black father from Kenya and a white mother from Kansas, Obama embodied the story. The media tried to understand him as they do everyone else in politics, as a progressive or a liberal or a conservative, but "America" is what Obama is about. The public understands that, or at least they did during his campaign, and Obama knew this. He knew that what was inside him was inside them—"America"—and whatever he said and did resonated from that point deep inside himself to that point deep inside them. His words sounded like *their* words, words they hadn't heard in a long time, words they didn't even know were still inside them, words they didn't know that they had been waiting to hear; words that made them feel that there is so much more in them as human beings, so much more in their country, so much more in their world. These Americans wanted to—and needed to— matter, and not only to themselves. They had known that about themselves, but something was reawakened in them during the Obama campaign. Life was not all about money; it was not all about things.

They wanted to feel *empowered*, that emotionless word that speaks of such an emotion-filled need. They needed somebody who was looking for the best in them.

It is easy to look for the worst and find it. Far harder and far more important is to seek out the best, appeal to the best, and bring out the best. People need that best in their own lives, and countries do too. But as a leader, you don't bring out that best only by highlighting its need. You have to set out tasks that demand it, and if you set the challenge bar too low and ask for little, you will receive little in return. For these Americans, it had been such a long time since anyone had asked something of them. And Obama sounded so touchingly naive when he did. He made important things seem possible. He made people want to try. He made people believe that perhaps the future can be different.

Obama sought out the best in the rest of the world too. He sent a message to the world's pariahs that he wanted to talk to them, to Iran's Ahmadinejad, Sudan's Bashir, and North Korea's Kim Jong-il. These leaders may deserve to be pariahs. It may feel good for us to make them pariahs, in that too rare moment of superiority we're unwilling to pass up. But this strategy hasn't worked well in the past. These leaders have been able to handle anything that the world has been willing to throw at them—economic sanctions, criminal charges from international courts, and words. Tightening the screws on them and on their countries has made them only more pariah-like. To invade their countries would be another matter. Ahmadinejad, Bashir, and Kim Jong-il know, however, that the rest of the world would not dare. These pariahs would make it too costly, too deadly, with too uncertain results, and if any of the world's countries did dare to cross their borders, the invasion itself would become the issue, and the invading countries would carry with them into the future the stain of being colonialists and imperialists and would never be trusted again. Other countries might one day see these invading countries as pariahs themselves and do the same to them.

When Obama sent out his message to these leaders, those experienced in the world saw it as one more sign of his weakness. This is not how the world works, they said. If you talk to these people, you give them a world audience; you legitimize them. But in Obama's reading of the world's history, of human nature, shutting off a rogue regime makes it only more rogue. Shutting off a fool only hides a fool. Letting a fool speak reveals a fool. By engaging these leaders, Obama believed, he would not legitimize them; they would de-legitimize themselves. He would act like "America" and do what other countries could not.

In September 2008, Ahmadinejad spoke at the United Nations. In January 2009, Obama, now U.S. president, announced he would reopen dialogue with Iran. In June 2009, after rigged elections in which Ahmadinejad had again been proclaimed president, millions of Iranians took to the streets, protesting day after day, the response of the government growing ever more violent.

Maybe things can be different, these Iranians believed. These three events were not unrelated, and there was a fourth event too. In October 2009, Obama was awarded the Nobel Peace Prize. The response from many in the United States, and from Obama himself, was one of surprise and embarrassment. Many others were angry. The prize was too much, or at least too soon, they said. In his nine months as president, what had he done? Yet there was little surprise in the rest of the world. It was the trips he had made and what he had said, in Cairo particularly, and how he had said it. The United States is part of the world, he told his audience, and the United States must think that way and act that way. But Obama's *real* impact came from his tone and from the respect he showed his audiences. He treated the other countries as if they mattered. All the rest—negotiations, agreements—could follow. All the rest now had a chance.

Slowly during the campaign, and little by little during the first months of his presidency, without even knowing it, the public was developing an immense stake in Obama, perhaps bigger than in any other U.S. president. People watched and waited for him to fail. They were certain that he would, and hoped that he wouldn't. They saw failure even when it was not there, and in doing so made failure more possible. They hoped so hard and feared so hard because if he did fail, imagine what that would say about America, and about the future. And who would take on the important issues now? Who would dare? Who would succeed? And why would the public ever believe anyone else who did try? Why would they believe that government could play any important role at all? Whether you are a Democrat or a Republican, whether you supported him or not, whether you agreed with him or not, one thing is undeniable: he is good. He has it all. If not him, who? If not in the United States, where? If not now, when?

During his first year as president, at times Obama had the look of a cartoon character being chased off a cliff, where, up in the air, with nothing visible beneath him, he just kept on running. And if, like a cartoon character, he kept on running and didn't look down, he *could* keep on running, discovering as he did that there was more in him and more in others than anyone had ever imagined; as if the cliff had wondrously extended out beneath him. For Obama, the cliff was the always-solid ground of "America."

WASHINGTON

WHEN U.S. PRESIDENT Barack Obama took on health care, everything began to change. When stuck in the mire of it, he seemed for a moment to doubt, to look down; the cliff no longer extending beneath him.

At times in that first year, he seemed to have a health-care deal, which had eluded every other president in American history and which should have made him look special in a way no other president had. At times, he didn't have a deal. Then at some moment, whether he had a deal or didn't have a deal mattered for the American people but didn't matter for Obama. All the debates, negotiations, and side deals had happened in what once would have seemed such an un-Obama-like way, so messy and rancorous, the worst of everyone on display, in the end his health-care provisions so immensely compromised. Fighting politics with politics, Obama had forgotten "America." In the midst of his fight for health care, he began to look like everyone else.

Then the late-night talk-show hosts began their amiable destruction. Until that time, Obama had represented a problem for them. He didn't have the same over-the-top exaggerations of most politicians. Although he liked to talk, he didn't speak as if he was the only person in existence. He liked attention, yet he didn't need to monopolize every eye and ear in every room he entered. He didn't grab you by the lapels and hold on to them until you loved him. He didn't make you want to resent him, or to hold back on him, or to punish him. He was likeable; he was hopeful; he was the first black president. It was extremely difficult to pick on him.

Then the talk-show hosts noticed that while Obama had put many important issues onto his plate, not much had come off it. He became to them "the Great Proclaimer," all "do" and no "done." As one of these hosts said, after many months, what was Obama's greatest accomplishment as president? Winning the Nobel Peace Prize.

When you are a president or a prime minister, it takes only one line, one phrase—out of thousands of posts a day—to define you, to set the angle on you, to create the target for thousands of others to shoot at daily. For the talk-show hosts, media, and bloggers, all this is such delicious fun. It is that chance in front of millions, or thousands, or a few, or only yourself to be smart, funny, never wrong, to show (jokingly, of course) how the powerful are such idiots.

This scenario has been Obama's life day after day, just as it is the life of any leader. There is the relentless chipping away at what you are, at how others see you, at what you want to do. There is the chipping away at how you see yourself, at the pride you must have, at the monumental confidence you need to take on important matters. Then, as leader, some day you flinch, you doubt, you look down. Then you laugh at yourself, to join the crowd to make yourself more likeable. You self-deprecate, likeably, as others deprecate you again and again.

All this time, the economy in the United States, as elsewhere, was struggling. The recession of 2009, which had felt much less bad than expected, had been followed by a recovery that felt much less good. Unemployment was still around 10 per cent, the highest in more than twenty-five years. The automobile industry, which had posted huge losses a year earlier, now posted lower losses or slight gains. Yet no one was fooled. In Afghanistan and Iraq, in Iran and Sudan, in North Korea and the Middle East, day-to-day matters seemed to change, but month to month they seemed not to. The American people, still seeing their country as the sole superpower in a superpower world, continued to express frustrated dismay at the power of seemingly powerless countries to do whatever they wanted to do. Being bigger and richer, being America, must count for something, they believed, and if it doesn't, it must be the fault of those in power. The failure is one of leadership, they said again and again, the failure of their president.

There have been some not-so-visible changes. Obama continues to travel abroad, to Japan, China, South Korea, Russia, and many other countries. He continues to talk respectfully; he continues to treat other countries as if they matter. The leaders of those countries, and especially their citizens, continue to react as if there is still a glow around him. These people remember the United States at other times; they remember other American presidents. Back at home, Americans watch the ceremony of Obama's trips. They see the same glow that others see around him, and yet they don't see any similar glow around the United States itself. Instead, the respect they see from other countries seems too casual, too arm-around-the-shoulders, too democratic, too much as if the United States is only an equal among equals. The other countries don't show the tiniest edge of fear that the weak ought to exhibit before the strong. Visit by visit, interaction by interaction, Obama is helping create a different global mood and respectfulness. All this is only of long-term effect, which, in the short term, doesn't seem like much to Americans. In Obama's time, as a partner in the world, the United States has been doing better; as a leader in the world, to Americans, it seems not.

In the days before Obama's State of the Union Address, the American people appeared to be building up to a national scream—health care, Afghanistan, bank bailouts, bank bonuses, Massachusetts Senate race, health care, bailouts, bonuses, politics! They were mad, mad at Obama, at America, at themselves, and at the world. They were mad at everything that had to do with politics: the scandals, the games, the big-shot preening by politicians in front of cameras and microphones. They were mad at the banks and at the bankers. As taxpayers, the American people had saved these bankers' asses: they had saved these bankers' jobs, their big fancy cars and yachts, their summer and winter houses, their "masters of the universe" smug faces. They had bailed out these people—the same people who had caused all this mess—with their own taxpayer money. If they had treated these bankers the way these bankers had always treated them—Uh, sorry, a loan?

Are you kidding? Look at your books!—they would
have thrown them out the door. Yet when the markets
improved, when the financial system began to stabilize,
after they as taxpayers had bailed them out, these
bankers acted as if nothing had happened, as if they
had done the turnaround all by themselves.

Before the State of the Union Address, it was bonus
time, and these large financial institutions were making
piles of money again. Yet there was no way these companies could go ahead and award their bonuses. They
wouldn't dare do that, for such an act would be too
brazen, too outrageous. After all, these bankers had
caused the problem in the first place. And with 9.7 per
cent of Americans, 14.8 million people, out of work,
with *no* paycheque in their pockets let alone bonuses,
with millions of them having lost their one and only
house, and with these same millions being among
those who had saved these bankers their jobs and cars
and houses—there was no way! They couldn't, they
wouldn't, yet they did: these bankers paid themselves
their bonuses in billions of dollars.

The bailout of the banks had saved the American financial system. Ten years from now and every year
after, that is how this moment will be remembered. But
not in January 2010, not before the State of the Union
Address. The bailout had brought about the bonuses,

and now the bailout was all about the bonuses. When people seek to hurt someone else in a way that will also hurt themselves, to bring them to their senses, we say to them, "Don't cut off your nose to spite your face." In this case, at this moment, if there had been no bailout, even if no bailout had meant harder times for these 14.8 million Americans, and even if many tens of millions of other Americans would have been thrown out of work; if no bailout had also meant that those bankers would have lost their jobs, houses, and inflated attitudes, millions and millions of Americans would have been willing to cut off their noses to spite their faces if only to cut off the noses of these bankers. This is how much they hated them.

In the midst of this national scream, Obama walked onto the floor of the House of Representatives to deliver his first State of the Union Address. Television commentators told us what they expected we would hear: a year-worn Obama, not contrite necessarily, but chastened from experience, willing to acknowledge his mistakes, willing to remove from his overflowing national agenda plate several issues, perhaps even health care, putting the focus on only a few issues, and principally the economy.

Obama began a little cautiously, a little defensively. He talked about the struggles Americans had faced throughout their history, and how Americans had responded. Their "stubborn resilience in the face of adversity," he described it, and the look on his face and the tone of his voice made it clear that, as president, he was determined to live up to that tradition, and he was sure that Americans would too. Obama took on the pettiness, the partisanship, and the "numbing weight" of politics, saying how Americans were tired of it and deserved better. The country had to get on with the future, he said, just as China, Germany, and India were doing. "How long should America put its future on hold?" Obama asked. "It's time to get serious."

Obama moved from one issue to another, mostly on matters of the economy, and as he finished with one, he would say, "Next . . ." building up the force of his comments as he spoke. Democratic Senators and Congressmen sitting in front of him and to his right stood and applauded every minute or so. In front and to his left, Republican Senators and Congressmen, except on rare occasions, remained seated and silent. It was like the Montreal Forum at the hockey game on the Saturday night before the Monday Quebec referendum in 1995, at the moment of the singing of "O Canada!" Who stood? Who sat? Who sang? Who did not? "We still need health insurance reform," Obama said finally to thunderous applause and to deafening silence. The problem

is not going away, and because it is not going away, he
told them, he will not go away either.

He returned to the matter of politics, the politics
of both Democrats and Republicans, to the destruc-
tiveness of a "perpetual campaign" where people
oppose anything "just because they can." To "just say
'no' is not leadership," he shouted. This task that
they both share, Democrats and Republicans, is not
about politics. This task has to do with their ideals
and values, "American values," he said. Do corpora-
tions, media, and government exhibit those values
today? he asked.

He talked for seventy minutes. He did not appear
year-worn. He was respectful and unchastened. He
acknowledged some mistakes, focused principally on
the economy, and removed little from his national
agenda plate, especially not health care. He was coolly
and confidently defiant. To Republicans, to Democrats,
to Americans, to his administration, maybe even to
himself, he reissued the challenge from his campaign,
the challenge to be "America."

In his State of the Union Address, Obama had done
what for many months he had stopped doing. During
these months he had talked, instead, to the issues of
the day—the economy, health care, climate change—
making smart points to debate his opponents in the

shriek-and-shrill of politics. He spoke to the issues; he did not speak to Americans. After the speech was over, one of Obama's former advisers and former Clinton chief of staff, John Podesta, said that in the previous months Obama had lost the narrative of what he had been trying to do, and with the State of the Union Address, he was trying to fit the pieces of that narrative together again. The narrative is "America." Americans are good, this narrative says. "America" makes them better.

During the campaign and at his best moments during the State of the Union Address, Obama seemed to preface every point about the economy or health care with: "This is America," spoken proudly, deter-minedly, and scoldingly too. "This is America"—we, not China, not Germany, not India, lead the way into the future. "This is America"—we have millions of our citizens who are one illness away from disaster. "This is America *for God's sake*"—we are Republicans and we are Democrats, but above all else we are Americans, and we will not put in the way, and we will not allow to have put in the way, anything that keeps us from being "America."

Most commentators found Obama's speech impres-sive. In their summations, they added, however, that the mid-term elections would occur in ten months' time. The Republicans smelled blood. Nothing much would change.

That night, many Americans became reacquainted with Obama. The larger question was whether Obama had become reacquainted with himself.

COPENHAGEN

A MONTH BEFORE U.S. president Barack Obama's State of the Union Address, the Copenhagen Conference took place. One hundred and ninety-three of the world's countries attended. The world's people, or many hundreds of millions of them—more people than pay attention to anything except Olympic Games or soccer World Cups—were watching. These are people whose thoughts and feelings are rarely able to stray far from their jobs and their families. Even the media seemed to sense that something elemental was happening.

Copenhagen followed the defining climate change conference at Kyoto. Twelve years had elapsed. Although there had been Bonn, The Hague, Marrakech, New Delhi, Milan, Buenos Aires, Montreal, Nairobi, Bali, and Poznan in between, these gatherings had been minor checkpoints along the way, all building to

Copenhagen. There had been twelve years of ice caps melting, glaciers disappearing, rain forests burning, polar bears starving, pine beetles engorging, and desert regions growing. These twelve years included 9/11, a South Asian tsunami, Hurricane Katrina, wars in Iraq and Afghanistan, Bush, a sub-prime meltdown, and crushing global recession, all to rivet attention away from ice caps, glaciers, and rain forests. There had been twelve years of China and India, and galloping, gobbling growth. There had been twelve years of science, the message of climate change finally penetrating into the mainstream. There had been twelve years of naively moving away from our selfish, worst selves toward our generous, best selves. There had been twelve years of climate change politics and climate change story. In the days before Copenhagen, all the world's other stories had come to seem mere distraction.

At Copenhagen, the world's leaders had hoped to sound like smart people offering smart ideas. But to the hundreds of millions who suddenly found themselves listening in a way they had never listened before, to the media who had found their own cynical wall penetrated in a way they were not ready for, these world leaders sounded stupid, so out of touch with science, so removed from what people were thinking and feeling. Why did these world leaders not understand? How could they not? Did they not realize that this was not just neighbours haggling over the backyard fence? This was our future; this was the planet. How could they not hear the thoughts of hundreds of millions of people screaming out, "No, no, you are not just negotiating this number or that. You are negotiating *me*, negotiating *my* life, *my* kids, *my* future. You have to know that. Tell me that you have a deal that will keep the seas from rising so my kids will have a future. Anything else and I'm not listening."

The public's reaction seemed to shock the world's leaders. Everything up until this moment at the conference had been so normal. In the first week, the bureaucrats had laid out their countries' positions, going as far as their instructions had allowed them to go, the media reporting on the "hopelessness" or the "hopefulness" of the conference, depending on the day. Then the ministers arrived, followed by the orchestrated protests in the streets by non-governmental organizations, fake press releases, and "Fossil of the Day" awards to embarrass the countries toward a better deal. Then, with two days to go and things looking bleak, the leaders arrived like the cavalry—Obama, Wen, Sarkozy, Brown. Their positions had been carefully put together. They wouldn't go so far as the one-issue advocates desired, of course, but they would stretch themselves farther than they had ever gone, farther even than they thought they could deliver. Then, with all the countries there in one place, with the pressure to please and the pressure to make a deal, they would go even farther. At the cliffhanger hour, they would make a deal. They would smile in triumph, gather for pictures, talk excitedly using words such as *unprecedented* and *historic*, then go home, leaving behind for the world a feeling that the worst of one more crisis had been averted. Life could go on.

But it didn't work out this way. The gaps between the world's countries, from massive China to the tiny Cook Islands, were too wide, their immediate realities too different. Most countries had done next to nothing to create the problem of climate change; a few had done a lot. Some had benefited economically from the creation of the problem, many almost not at all. One country, the United States, had done more and had benefited more than anyone in the past, and would do more and benefit more in the future. Another country, China, had done little and had benefited little in the past but would do more and benefit far more in the future. And all the countries would share climate change's wrath, though some island nations, including the Maldives and Tuvalu, which had done little and benefited even less, might face extinction altogether. Who should pay the real cost of climate change?

When no agreement was reached, organizers extended the conference several hours. Obama went about from leader to leader being Obama. But more hours, even more days, wouldn't have made a difference. The leaders weren't even close to any kind of substantive agreement. All that was left was to agree on whatever was agreeable and to find some language open and broad and indefinite enough to allow any country to do a lot if it wanted, and much less if it had no such desire. Then the leaders would smile, gather for pictures, talk excitedly, use a phrase such as "of course, more work needs to be done," call the gathering a "success," and go home.

For the large economic powers, the key was to get everyone out of town—if there were no actors, there was no stage; if there were no stage, there was no drama. For a few days, that tactic seemed almost to work. If the leaders were not there, the media had no reason to be there and the non-governmental organizations weren't interesting enough on their own. Moreover, the leaders—they had all been there!—had tried, and the whole world had seen that. They had come together and held the world's attention for two weeks. They had signalled to one and all that now and forever climate change is a major world problem. The leaders had done their best. Back home, they would continue to work on it. Surely even all the sideline geniuses could see that more was now not possible. And there would be the next meeting in Mexico City in another year.

The media quickly moved on; the leaders of the world's biggest countries moved on; many of the public and many other countries did not. The global story of climate change and the global politics of Copenhagen had come together for everyone to see. Before the conference began, stories were published that questioned the validity of some of the climate change findings. A server was hacked, and thousands of emails and other documents were leaked that purported, among other things, to show that climate scientists had manipulated and withheld scientific data and suppressed dissenting scientific papers. These improper actions were the result of simple mistakes, some said, or they were because of people who believed too strongly in their own story, or they were because of people who, with a bigger agenda to change the world, needed the imminence of climate change to do that. If the right information had been included, some said, the impact on the projections would have been minor, or, others said, the projections would have changed altogether. But the answers did not matter. Doubt was enough. The leaders did not make a deal at Copenhagen because they did not need to make a deal. A month after the conference had ended, that was the story of Copenhagen.

At the time, however, this was not the story of Copenhagen. During the conference, the story had been that, faced with a global problem that put human life at risk, faced with the future of a species, faced with a global problem that only the world's countries *together* could answer, the world's leaders at Copenhagen had to make a major ambitious deal. Yet they couldn't do it. Even with all that was on the line, *they couldn't do it.* The global story of climate change couldn't meet the challenge of the global politics of Copenhagen. That, not climate change or the disputed numbers of climate change, was the story of Copenhagen.

Global politics had won in Copenhagen just as American national politics had won in the United States. The story of climate change and the story of "America" had proven no match. But the voice of politics was now not the only voice present. Before Obama, before Copenhagen, it had seemed acceptable for a citizen to react from the sidelines to the external things in their lives. Governments were going to do what governments were going to do. Nothing could stop them. But for many, this reality is no longer good enough. Governments cannot be allowed to do what they have always done because the consequences are too great. After Obama, after Copenhagen, more people are beginning to fight back. "I am not a spectator," they are saying, "and I will not let you make me be a spectator. This is my life, my future, my kids' future."

Islands disappearing under rising waters, the shorelines of great coastal cities pushed inland permanently, people pushed out—Hurricane Katrina was our cautionary tale. Imagine a hundred Katrinas. Imagine thousands and thousands of people unable to stay where they are and with nowhere to go. Imagine millions of people affecting hundreds of millions more, affecting billions more. It is not possible that we are powerless, that we cannot make a deal on climate change. It is not possible that we cannot overcome our politics, both international and national, and that we are unable to stop ourselves from heading down a path that can end only in one place. We are human beings. We evolved a capacity to think—to analyze, to understand, to act. By working together, we can survive. We can stop. And we refuse to let anyone make us believe it is impossible.

Changing gears is not easy. We used to think that the answer to any problem was awareness. The answer was seeing problems so clearly and in such dramatic dimension that suddenly, filled with outrage and laden with guilt, there was no way we could do anything but generate the will needed to solve those problems. But seeing what is wrong is not enough; seeing what is wrong is easy; and seeing what is right is easy too. Our libraries are filled with books by experts who make their case forcefully page after page, chapter after chapter, of what is wrong and what is right, as if to put off the inevitable, a final chapter where they have no choice but to confront the question: "How, then, do we make things right?" Then, in a few pages, they offer their answer, which looks so embarrassingly trite even to their own eyes, and so unsatisfying to everyone else's. Preferring right to trite, they then scurry back to right and continue a case already made.

Seeing what is right is easy; finding the road from wrong to right is hard. It is the same with vision. "Where are the leaders with 'vision?'" we plead again and again. But vision is easy too. What is difficult is finding the story that produces that vision, that is credible, that is worthy of believing, that inspires action. Just as a punchline to a joke has no punch without its story, a vision without its story has no punch. Without its story, a vision is stuck by itself in the middle of nowhere, like a neon light in the desert with no roads to get from here to there.

We used to think the answer was trying harder—"Where there's a will, there's a way." It is one of our favourite exhortations. But will is not enough. As with awareness and rightness and vision, will is easy. Will is being hopeful, will is being a "glass-half-full" person, will is working hard and not giving up. But "will" without "way" gets frustrated, and like Sisyphus and his rock, it ends up nowhere. With big, challenging problems, in fact, the truth is far more often the reverse: "Where there's a way, there's a will."

Once, it seemed, the news media were part of the answer. It was their job to see what was wrong and to ensure that the public saw what was wrong, the decision-makers, both government and corporate, saw what was wrong, and to demand that those decision-makers fix the problem. As newspapers became bigger and with broader reach, with radio, television, and the Internet, the news media were able to see more and more wrong. Seeing wrong is easy. All they had to do was close their eyes, point in any direction, open their eyes, follow their finger, and there was always something embarrassingly wrong.

That is all that media needed to do. Then the decision makers, the government mostly, would take that information and do right. Except doing right, as we know, is far harder than being right, and being right is far more fun. The most fun of all is being right with a twist. So being right with a twist has become the rage, and for the media too.

Irony is the prevailing attitude of our age. At its best, irony reveals truths when straight-ahead messages cannot. Irony sticks a timely pin into us to keep us from getting too full of ourselves. For those aspects of life that are hard to make right, irony also keeps us at arm's length from hoping the hopeless and feeling its irremediable pain.

In today's world, irony is everything we have come to love; it seems clever, and is always right and funny. Delivered without emotional commitment, it comes with no risk of pain. It makes the ironist the smartest person in the room and more important than whatever the ironist is supposed to be speaking about. Letterman and Leno, Colbert and Stewart, Walsh and Feschuk are funny, but they aren't talking about Obama and McCain, Harper and Ignatieff, climate change and economic meltdowns. They are talking about themselves. Irony is about "me." *The world is wrong; I can't make it right, so I see myself as better than the world. It is how I live with myself.* In an ironic world, the medium is not the message. The messenger is the message.

Irony offers distraction and escape. It allows us to ridicule those who take on the hard stuff, like climate change, who believe and try. Irony is giving up. As a diversion, it is wonderful. As the attitude of an age, it is a disaster. We live in a post-ironic world, and a post-ironic world is about "us."

In 2008, Americans voted for Obama because giving up doesn't work. They wanted to believe in Obama, and they wanted to believe in America. They wanted to believe that there was a lot more good in themselves, more than they knew and more than anyone knew. And Americans loved how that made them feel when they found it. Obama was going to take on important matters, and he needed the American people. For so long they had been ready for their government to ask more of them, but nobody had. To politicians, it seemed wrong to ask for help from those who pay your salary, and whose votes you need. But, of course, it isn't. There is a reason that the most resonant American presidential phrase of the twentieth century was John Kennedy's "Ask not what your country can do for you. Ask what you can do for your country." The biggest compliment of our time is that a person "makes a difference." It is a message that says to each of us that in a world of nearly 7 billion people, it matters that we exist.

We act in our own self-interest, and self-interest is almost always understood as economic. Money leads, and we follow. A more reliable predictor of behaviour is purpose. If we want to predict what people will do, find out what matters to them. Follow "the purpose," not "the money." For some, money is the purpose. And if it's not money directly, it's money as the main instrument to realize that purpose—a house to call your own, a new car, things that make you feel successful. But now many people are looking for something more.

Once, people found purpose in religion. Beyond the routine of their lives, they found a bigger purpose, to serve God, to do His will on Earth, and in doing so to live through all eternity. Religion had been a way to explain everything around them—good and bad, happiness and sadness, life and death—to make the unknown seem known, to make it predictable, as if to put it under some human control.

Then science offered a better explanation, though without a built-in larger purpose, without God, and without life everlasting. Some came to find purpose in their work, some in people, some in money and things; some found no need for any external purpose at all. Some sought out purpose in themselves. *God offered me eternal life if I made others matter more than me. God died. I matter most.* Many others, discovering that they needed purpose and not finding it, have now turned back to religion. Many now seek more intense evangelical experiences. Others reject the formalities and institutions of religion for spirituality, worshipping life and all its forces and mysteries.

Still others find the bigness, other-ness, and meaning they need in "the Planet": something that is also unfathomably vast, unknowable, the source of everything, and in human terms, lasting for eternity; the Planet, as if it were God in concrete form. Its atoms and molecules give us life, its air and water sustain us—this is the Planet, and without it we wouldn't exist. For many, climate change and its risks to the Planet drive this new environmentalism. It is almost a religion itself, very much like Aboriginal understandings, with Nature or the Planet at the centre. This environmentalism is especially powerful for the young, who believe in themselves, in the possibilities of their own lives, and in the future. It is also powerful in those over the age of sixty, who had started believing in the 1960s. They had thought they could do away with war and racism and have peace and love forever; they became embarrassed by life as life came to be, and they turned their backs on their old/young selves, though they never forgot what believing had felt like. Now, these older people are back because they can see the end of their own time, because they can see life everlasting only in the lives of their children and grandchildren, and only on a sustainable Planet.

As the Planet becomes more at risk, as "end of the world" scenarios become more credible and more depictions of it hit our movie screens, people are wanting to believe. They need to believe, and there is desperation in their quest that was not present before. Doom is easy, but doom doesn't get us anywhere. We are more than this because we need to be more than this.

It is the need to believe, the need to take on the important matters, the need to find meaning and purpose, the need to come together on something more important than ourselves that is now driving the people of the Planet toward something more purposeful than money. And this new drive is giving the world a chance in a time of climate change. This common global understanding, this common global culture based on the Planet, offers possibility. This is not a religion to replace other religions; it is something separate. In the beginning, it was religion that explained the planet and gave us our meaning and purpose. Now it is the Planet that gives meaning and purpose itself.

The world is different now than it was a few years ago. It is time for the "how," not the "what"; for the "way," not the "will"; for doing right, not being right; for the "us," not the "me"; for purpose, not politics; for the passionists who write stories, not the ironists who critique them; for the aspirational, not the cautionary; for the possibility, not the doom.

Standing resolutely in the way is the cynicism and the irony of politics.

OTTAWA I

Liberals Lose. Harper Wins.

IN CANADA, WE HAVE BEEN witness to the stories of Obama and of Copenhagen, of people hopeful and mad and much changed by their experiences, yet no Obama-style leaders of our own have emerged. No major political party has changed its long-standing traditional directions. To Canadians, once again, the Obama phenomenon has seemed to be something that happens in the United States because things like this do happen in the United States. Things like this don't happen here because we are *just* Canada. Before changes like this can happen in Canada, we would have to matter more, and first we would have to matter more to ourselves.

For our 143-year existence as a country, this has been our understanding of ourselves—"we are just Canada." But not now, not entirely. A different feeling is emerging, one expressed mostly in private conversation, one we didn't even notice for so long and we didn't dare trust. This feeling couldn't possibly be right, and because it couldn't be right, we didn't talk about it, and because we didn't talk about it, it couldn't be inside others and wasn't inside ourselves. The feeling comes from being bigger. It comes from many millions of people new to Canada who don't know the old stories of Canada and only know what they see. The feeling comes from people who aren't preoccupied with what they are supposed to be and just do amazing things—writers, musicians, athletes, architects, inventors, business people—in Canada or across borders; to them, it doesn't matter. "We are not what we were told we are," they express in everything they do. "We are more than this."

In Canada, as opposed to the United States, politics has played little role in this national reconsideration. In fact, in Canada, politics has gotten in the way. The one party that might have been important to such developments, the Liberals, has been for many years out of synch with the times. Gaining power in 1993 at a time of recession and high deficit, the Liberals took on the deficit as a mission, pushing to one side their traditional social justice priorities. When deficits turned to surpluses by the late 1990s, fiscal management had become the Liberals' new point of pride, and they decided not to put it at risk by returning to their traditional priorities. Then scandal and governing fatigue drove them from office in 2006.

Conservative Party prime minister Stephen Harper sees politics, government, and Canada differently. He grew up in the kind of suburb that only a decade before had produced a generation raised on the immense future of post-war Canada. Harper's generation arrived in the ebb of this wave, seeing less the possibilities of Canada and more what it was then—successful, prosperous, relatively small, doing fine, and doing so in an American-centred world that would always be an American-centred world. And what was wrong with that? Harper came to believe overwhelmingly in personal freedoms, which no one and nothing had the right to impinge on, the most likely culprit, of course, being that which had the greatest power—government. He had seen too often government's great schemes, the National Energy Program most particularly, dressed up as actions for "the good of the country," which, to him, were only expressions of the personal dreams of those who had gotten their hands on government and were using government for their own purposes, at great cost—in taxes paid and freedoms lost—to everyone else. To Harper, government was at most a small and limited necessary evil, and taxes were money far better off left in people's pockets to spend as they saw fit.

How one would deal with schools or a health-care system or affordable housing or roads, those things that are also central to a nation's success—and that are difficult to build and grow one pocket at a time—Harper has never said.

Harper doesn't talk much about the country itself and what we might be. He is distrustful of hopes and dreams. Hopes and dreams are too easily manipulated and too easily turn one's head. To him, setting the bar at a four and hitting a four is a success; setting it at an eight and hitting a seven, a failure. Aspirations are for people, not for governments. What he despises most are those whose stock and trade are hopes and dreams. That is what the Liberals do: they dream dreams beyond what they can deliver, then they appeal to those same dreams inside Canadians, obtain their support, win elections much of the time, yet never deliver on all that they dream. It doesn't matter to Harper that dreams are just that, dreams, not all of which are ever realized—that is how life is—and people understand and accept that. It doesn't matter to him that dreaming dreams has also produced medicare, old age pensions, a national railway system, peacekeeping, and a Charter of Rights and Freedoms. To him in his pinched way, this governmental dreaming, with such uncertain results, is wrong. When the Liberals ran out of dreams

credible even to themselves after thirteen years of government, Canadians gave Harper his chance.

Harper has governed in a manner entirely faithful to
himself. That has not always seemed the case to some
of his most ideological supporters, who criticize him
for governing too often "toward the centre," especially during the recession, when he has spent immense
amounts of taxpayers' money trying to stimulate the
economy and amassing the highest deficit in Canadian
history. Whenever he seems to stray, however, he has
only done so kicking and screaming and not for long. It
is only when circumstances have generated an overwhelming public clamour for action—on the recession,
on climate change—that Harper has done what he
doesn't believe, and then only to the minimum degree.
He has learned, too, that what any government does is
so difficult to understand—and with a little spin so
easy to make confusing—that on those issues where he
knows the public is demanding big action, he can do
much less, talk the language of more, and no one will
know enough with sufficient certainty to have the confidence forcefully to oppose him. He can do small and spin
big to give the public what it wants, and he can still be
true to himself and manage himself through the day.

Obama represents what Harper distrusts. Obama
dreams too big even for America. Worst of all, so much

of what he dreams needs to be government-centred and government-driven. When governments think they can do almost anything, Harper believes, they are wrong and they become dangerous. In his big-dreaming ways, Obama might infect too easily impressionable Canadians.

After the 2008 American election, Harper exhibited nothing but respect for Obama. Obama was, after all, the president of the United States. When the recession hit hardest, when banks were failing and American car companies were about to go under, Harper waited for Obama to act. Our economies are so tied, he reasoned, waiting is the responsible thing to do. But he also knew that Obama would have to do about spending what Harper and his most ideological supporters could never bring themselves to do alone. The same situation existed with climate change. On climate change, Harper would not have to act in ways that hurt Alberta's tar sands and its economy unless the United States threatened to act against the tar sands first. In Obama's first months as president, Harper did what he had no choice but to do and he let the rest drift. He never challenged Obama, hoping that Obama's glow would fade and political reality would return. Then Harper could go back to something more comfortable. Harper hoped to wait out Obama.

Waiting out Obama would have been far harder for Harper except for the wrong-footedness of the Liberals. When a party becomes the government, it brings with it what it believes in and is proud to represent. Then day after day, month after month, year after year, facing a political opposition, media, and public who shakes their heads and rolls their eyes at virtually everything it does, a government loses its confidence and faith in what it is doing, it loses its sense of direction, and it knows no longer what it should be proud of and why it matters that it is the government. And if it cannot feel proud of itself and what it believes in, it cannot persuade a public that it should be the government. So it loses, and in losing, it has a chance to rediscover itself.

For the Liberals, this scenario took more than twelve years to play out in part because of the governing genius of the Liberals and much more so because of the disintegration of the Progressive Conservatives. In 1984, the Progressive Conservatives had won the support of disaffected Liberals in Quebec and in Western Canada, making Brian Mulroney the new prime minister. The Progressive Conservatives lost that support, and more, when wiped out by Jean Chrétien's Liberals nine years later. Both Quebec and the West have long felt themselves cut off from power in Canada. For Quebec, despite being the second most populous province, and despite Quebeckers holding the office of prime minister and other high Cabinet positions with great frequency, this is because of its minority language reality, because of historic slights and unfairnesses, because of feeling forever "other." For the West, it is because of its relatively small population and correspondingly small number of seats compared to the central Canadian giants of Ontario and Quebec. So Quebec and the West, no matter what government is in power, never believe themselves represented at the centre and are always ready to support someone new until there is someone new; then, with the realities of population and power unchanging, decade after decade, government after government, they always feel left out. The cyclical fatigue of the nine-year-old Mulroney government and the relative weakness of the Chrétien Liberals brought about the seismic shift that followed.

The Mulroney government had run its course, and the public wanted a change. Normally in such a case, the disaffected, or at least a high percentage of them, would have returned ritually to the Liberals as the only other party that could form the government. But this time, feeling no connection to the Progressive Conservatives and still feeling none to the Liberals, the disaffected did not return. After years of talk and nothing else, protest parties formed. In Quebec, the Bloc Québécois, whose central mandate was an independent Quebec, was led by Lucien Bouchard. Nationally, but principally in the West, the Reform Party was led by Preston Manning. In the 1993 election, the Bloc won 54 of 75 seats in Quebec; the Reform Party won 24 out of 32 seats in British Columbia, and 22 out of 26 in Alberta. The Bloc became the Official Opposition, just ahead of the Reform Party, the New Democratic Party was reduced to 9 seats, the Progressive Conservatives, which had gone into the election as a majority government with 169 seats, won only 2 seats. Yet had the Liberals been stronger, much of the Progressive Conservatives' support would have shifted to them, making it unlikely that the Bloc or the Reform Party would ever have been created. But with 177 seats and facing more parties that had only fragmented support, the Liberals' political weakness now looked like overwhelming governing strength.

And quickly, that is how the Liberals' weakness was perceived. Battles are won by the victorious, not lost by the vanquished, no matter what the truth, and this fact becomes only more the truth with every year that passes. People like heroes; we prefer winners to losers. And how the battle is won becomes the conventional wisdom for how every battle needs to be won in the future, with the generals who offered the conventional wisdom that guided the victory becoming now and forever the conventionally wise. In time, for the Liberals, all this would be the bad news wrapped up in the good news.

The recession of 1993 hit especially hard because of a fiscal deficit then approaching $40 billion a year. Now in power, the Liberals had no governing options, only a governing necessity. Their central social justice strategy had to be their central economic strategy, which had to be their central fiscal strategy: lower the deficit to generate the confidence to encourage the investment, to drive the economy, to create the jobs, to lessen the number of those in need, and to do more for those who still need more help. The private sector also cut back, firing for the first time in a systematic way the educated and highly skilled who had never been unemployed before and who had thought never in their lives would be unemployed. Now finding themselves out in the cold, like animals raised in captivity suddenly set loose, they had no idea what to do. The federal government cut jobs and services almost across the board— social transfers to the provinces, business subsidies, defence, forty-five thousand jobs eliminated in the federal civil service. With less money, the federal government cut transfers to the provinces and territories, and now with less money, the provinces and territories in turn cut transfers to the municipalities.

The strategy worked far better and far sooner than even the Liberal government had imagined. The recession ended, and Canada was now in a fiscal position to benefit. Economic growth generated increased employment and increased tax revenues, which shrunk deficits and finally generated surpluses. By 2005, Canada was the only country in the G8 in surplus, and had been in surplus for nine straight years. Our fiscal performance was better than that of the United Kingdom, France, and Germany, better than Italy, Russia, and Japan, better even than the United States. As a government, the Liberals had achieved something substantial. Forget the political hammering and spin, reality was there in the numbers. Canada's fiscal surplus was a story that could be told and could stand for a lot of other stories much harder to tell. For the Liberal government, this surplus became *the* point of pride.

And the Liberals kept winning. Their majority was reduced in the 1997 election, the result, it seemed, of the usual accumulation of unpopular positions and general public sourness inherent in governing. The Reform Party, the New Democratic Party, and the Progressive Conservatives slightly increased their seat totals, enough for the hopeful among them to continue along in their hopeful trap; the Bloc went down a little but not enough to discourage them or their supporters.

Yet the story of the 1997 election had been about the continued disarray of the opposition parties, and the continued disaffection with the Liberals in Quebec and the West. The result was a political *status quo*, which brought out the worst in everyone.

When a party or a team wins, they hold together because they know if they don't hold together, they might lose. When they lose, they hold together because they know they must hold together to give themselves a chance to win. But when they seem too weak to win, they fight among themselves to find some better way. And why not? They will lose anyway. And if they seem too strong to lose, they fight among themselves. And why not? They will win anyway. So year after year the Reform Party, the Progressive Conservatives, and eventually the Canadian Alliance (which was formed out of the Reform Party in 2000) fought among themselves because they were too weak to win. And year after year, the Liberals, both the Chrétien supporters and the Martin supporters, fought among themselves because they were too strong to lose. Then the conservative parties broke their habit, came together, and won.

In 2003, the Progressive Conservative Party and the Reform/Canadian Alliance Party merged to become the Conservative Party, with Stephen Harper as leader. Its supporters were divided on many things—ideology, geography, tone, attitude—but Harper reminded them, and kept reminding them, of what they held absolutely in common. They hated the Liberals. For them, the words most often used to describe the Liberals didn't quite capture what they felt. It wasn't that the Liberals acted "entitled"—in the infamous phrase of once Liberal Cabinet minister David Dingwall, who, when questioned about his expense accounts, responded, "I'm entitled to my entitlements." Or that the Liberals understood themselves as Canada's "natural governing party." The Conservatives' feeling was more visceral. It was the Liberals' smugness. The Liberals thought they were so smart. *They* are city; we are country. *They* are manufacturing; we are raw materials. *They* are East; we are West. *They* are where the country happens; we are not. *They* are . . . superior; we are not. The Liberals would never say that, of course; that would be too "illiberal" of them. But the Conservatives could feel their dismissive message. And the Liberals always won.

What has stuck deep into the Conservatives' craw is the gun registry, as deeply as the National Energy Policy but more broadly across the country. With the gun registry, here were all these city people who knew nothing about guns except what they had seen on television, who hated guns and were scared to death of guns, and who, in their intellectual way, thought guns were "just wrong" because criminals in their cities could get guns and kill people. Here in the country were all these unsophisticated "hicks" who knew lots about guns because they had lived with them almost every day of their lives, who weren't scared of guns and didn't hate them, and who respected guns and knew how to handle them. Now they are handed this gun registry, and the Liberals are surprised when these "hicks" will not and cannot accept that if they don't register their guns they will be considered by the law to be "criminals." We might be a lot of things, they thought, but we cannot and will not accept anyone, especially from the cities, especially from "the East," especially "Liberals," calling us criminals. And if they make us criminals with their laws, we will do far more than just argue back. We will hate them.

Then there was Trudeau, the Liberals' patron saint. Conservative supporters/Liberal haters admired him, too, in many ways. When he stepped onto the world stage, he made us feel proud. He was smart. Suddenly the moment was not about our 25 million people and their 250 million people, nor about their glorious past and present and our small and modest existence. This was about our Trudeau and their Nixon, or Carter, or Reagan, or Thatcher, or Brezhnev, or Mao. And he was as smart as they were, maybe smarter. He was as good, maybe better, and that made us as good, maybe better, than them.

But on our own stage, in Canada, Trudeau made Conservative supporters/Liberal haters feel small. Everything about him said to them, "Why can you not be like me?" Smart like me, speak perfectly accented French and English like me. They would respond, But we didn't have a French-Canadian father and a Scottish- and French-Canadian mother. We didn't live where French was spoken. We didn't live a life of privilege in Montreal. We didn't go to the best schools. We didn't travel the world. We didn't spend our twenties and thirties and most of our forties doing whatever we wanted to do. We couldn't be like him. He didn't inspire us to do more, to be more, to do great things. He was of a different world. Instead, he made us feel inferior, re- minding us of what we aren't and what we can't be. For those who were enough like him to imagine themselves like him, maybe they were inspired. Maybe they were brought to aspire to more, and did more. But not for many Canadians, not in the West, nor even in Quebec, these Conservative supporters/Liberal haters would say. Many in Quebec still despise him to this day. And if you didn't agree with him, they would continue, he shrivelled you with his eyes, his words, his tone. "How can you be so stupid?" he seemed to say. "What is wrong with you?"

For Harper and his supporters, there was so much about the Liberals not to like. Harper may be a Conservative. He may believe in small government. He may believe in low taxes. He may believe government is of little use. But more than being a Conservative, he is a "not-Liberal." He does not like "liberal" ideas, and even more he hates absolutely the Liberal Party.

The Liberal Party has been the government of Canada for most of Canada's history, and Harper knows that for the Conservatives to take power, defeating the Liberals in any single election is not enough. That has happened many times before, and always the Liberals have kept coming back and for much longer stretches than the Progressive Conservatives. This election success was not only because Canada is a more "liberal" country, Harper believes, but because Canada is a more "Liberal" country too. Political affiliation is partly habit—the longer you affiliate with one party, the longer you will continue to affiliate with it—people become comfortable and like to back winners. For anything to change, he believes, Canadians needed to develop more "conservative" *and* more "Conservative" habits of mind. For that to happen, the Conservatives needed to win government more often and for longer periods of time. For that to happen, the Liberals must be defeated. For the Liberals to be defeated, they must be destroyed.

It is with this consistency of mind that Harper has governed. And because of this consistency, he has not so much governed as he has campaigned never-endingly, because it is only by remaining the government, by creating this habit, that he can achieve what he needs to achieve. At times he has seemed oddly conciliatory— on Afghanistan. At times, he has seemed oddly intransigent—on anti-terrorism legislation. But there is nothing odd or inconsistent about either of his actions. He could see differences within the Liberal Party on Afghanistan that his conciliation would exacerbate, and so he was conciliatory. He could see differences on the anti-terrorism sunset clause that his intransigence would exacerbate, and so he was intransigent. His direction was not determined by ideology or by pragmatic belief, but by the opportunity to weaken and weaken further the Liberal Party.

In bringing the opposition conservative parties together, Harper had given the newly constituted Conservative Party a bigger purpose, something that, even in government, the Liberals had lost. It is not enough of a purpose for a party only to stay in power. Every party needs something outside of itself, bigger than itself, that matters more to itself even than it does as a party. Every party needs something that makes it feel good and gives it energy, something that can be explained to others to make them excited, for party members then to see that excitement, feel proud, and get excited themselves. The Liberals had lost this purpose and pride, even if their general directions and beliefs remained those of the majority of the Canadian people; even if they had implemented some policies worthy of pride that were important enough to stay in place and to affect millions of lives for decades to come—the National Child Benefit, the Canada Research Chairs, same-sex marriage, the rejection of bank mergers, the rejection of engagement in Iraq; and even if they had put into place the beginnings of other policies—the Kelowna Accord, national early learning, and child care—that might have had a similar impact but for their cancellation by the Conservatives after the Conservatives' victory in 2006. There still seemed to be about the Liberals an absence of conviction, an absence of direction and coherence, as if tactics had taken over, where as a party you take one action and make it seem like another until you don't even know yourself which is which anymore. What, then, are you? And you come not to know. You hold on to your liberal beliefs, but you stop finding ways of explaining to yourself why you act as you act. You stop trusting your own words. Worse still, you lose your liberal habit. You just do, and you hope that what you do adds up to some semblance of what you want to do, and keeps you in power.

In truth, it had been a long time since Liberals had acted and felt like liberals. Perhaps the last best time had been in 1982 with the passage of the Charter of Rights and Freedoms. After that, Trudeau and his successor, John Turner, had limped along in power until the party was swept out in 1984, where it remained for nine years, before returning to government during a recession that offered few liberal opportunities. Then the Chrétien years and (briefly) the Martin years. National unity offered a focus in the mid-1990s, but after the Meech Lake and Charlottetown negotiations, where new visions of the country had been presented and rejected, what was left was the negative, near-disastrous fight of the 1995 Quebec referendum. Indeed in 1995, different from 1980, the national unity question held little interest for many, even in Quebec, until the referendum itself gave it interest. If a referendum is to be held, if as a citizen you are asked, on the whole, what side of the *fédéraliste-indépendentiste* line you fall, even if that question is not the first priority in your mind, you need to have an answer. And your expressed answer seems like your expressed priority, even if it is some-body else's priority and not your own. Indeed after the referendum vote and other than during the Clarity Act debate, despite the almost inconceivable 94 per cent of Quebeckers who had voted and the breathtaking narrowness of the *fédéraliste* victory, 50.58 per cent to 49.42 per cent, the national unity question fell to the nether regions on the political radar of the country, even in Quebec, where it has remained in the years since. During the latter years of their more than a decade in power, the Liberals, the "national unity party" of Canada, would find in national unity only brief focus, and not the purpose they needed.

The Liberals needed a purpose not only because the country needed the energy and excitement a purpose brings, but also to have something to fixate on besides themselves. Sitting around a table, if you have nothing big and compelling on that table to focus on, you will focus on each other. If you have nothing external to fight for, you will find something internal to fight for and against—each other. But for the Liberals, what did it matter? With a majority victory in 1993, a lesser majority in 1997, and a larger majority again in 2000, they were too strong to lose. Even if they weren't, with the Bloc doing worse and the Reform (now the Canadian Alliance), the New Democrats, and

Progressive Conservatives going nowhere, the others were too weak to win. Prime Minister Jean Chrétien was the most popular federal figure in the country, or his finance minister, Paul Martin, was. At some point, Martin would replace Chrétien, the Liberals would win a greater or a lesser majority; nothing else was at issue. So many Liberals, too many Liberals, focused on the only issue at play—the "when": when Chrétien would leave, when Martin would take over—and the divisions in the party grew wider.

This misdirected focus might not have mattered much if things had continued to go well. If the economy had kept strong, which it did, if the conservative parties had remained apart. Then, no matter the Liberals' internal fight, Martin would have become prime minister and would have continued as prime minister for two full terms at least. In the face of this new power, the resentful and disaffected Chrétien-ites would have drifted away unheard or irrelevant, or feeling a need to continue as political players, they would have swallowed their anger and made their peace. Attracted by power, new Martin loyalists would enter the scene to replace them. But nothing goes well forever. The question is always what you do when a situation turns. In this case, the turn came with the Sponsorship Scandal and the subsequent Gomery Commission's inquiry.

An inquiry offers to opposing political parties and to the media something new every day: a new witness, the same witness asked new questions, some fresh excuse for media to be present with media's need to fill space or time. Whatever else might be the news about a government that day doesn't have a chance. And coming day after day, such news becomes what a government is about. This news can define a government, especially if the details of the scandal don't seem too much of a stretch from what the public has already sensed about that government. It is all politics anyway, it seems to the public, that insider's game where people reward each other, where those in power get corrupted and those in power longer get corrupted more. And here are the Liberals, in power so long, acting "entitled" again. For the public, it becomes time to teach the Liberals a lesson. Nothing else the Martin government did ever received much attention. The health-care deal with the provinces and territories, the infrastructure deals with the cities, the recurring surpluses, the Kelowna Accord, the child-care deals— they all played out to the public at a decibel level of 50; Gomery was at 100. All those years of bland liberalism, of policies too infrequent or too modest to give the government identity and definition, could not stand up to the power of Gomery. Knocked down day after day, Paul Martin didn't have in place enough visible achievements ever to get himself off the floor. And if you don't have enough of yourself in your own window for the public to see, you risk someone else filling your window with something of their own.

Although the Canadian people still felt no strong reasons to vote for Stephen Harper, they had run out of reasons to vote Liberal. In January 2006, they voted in a new minority Harper government.

In 2006, if the Liberals had genuinely believed that Canada would be better off with a Liberal government, and if they had genuinely believed that child care, Kelowna, and Kyoto mattered, they wouldn't have fought among themselves and brought themselves down. If they had genuinely believed, they forgot.

There are 308 ridings in the country. One person can vote only in one riding for one local candidate. Occasionally a voter will vote principally with a local candidate in mind, more often with a party, most often with a party leader who would become the prime minister. In the 2006 election, there were 14,817,159 separate and individual decisions made; none of them involved a direct vote for prime minister. On election day, in the polling booth, imagine if the Canadian people had been offered a choice, not of candidates, but of the following scenario:

We are ready for a change. We are still not sure about Stephen Harper; we don't like him much, and we aren't sure we trust him. On the whole, we prefer the Liberals to the Conservatives, but the Liberals have been the government too long and need time out of power to rediscover themselves, to find their energy and purpose again, then to come back to us with the best that is in them. So we want to deliver a message to them and to Harper too. We are willing to make Harper the prime minister, but we will only give him a weak minority government, to keep him from being the worst that we fear is in him, and to keep the Liberals within striking distance for the next time.

If Canadians had been given that choice, the great majority of them would have voted for it. Somehow from those 14,817,159 separate, individual decisions cast in big cities and small towns, in the east and west and north, cast by people who would never vote Liberal or Conservative or New Democrat or Bloc, or who always do, or who might . . . depending—remarkably, unbelievably, out of all that, on January 23, 2006, the great majority of Canadians received what they wanted. And the result would prove worse for the Liberals than anyone could imagine.

OTTAWA II

Minority Government

WHEN A PARTY LOSES to a minority government, the good news is that an election might happen at any time and the losing party might not stay out of power for long. The bad news is that an election might happen at any time so the party never gets out of tactical political mode and never refinds those policy directions, and people, that might make it proud and electable again. Since the 2006 election, the Liberals have seemed always on the edges of the game and never back in it.

At first for the Liberals, being in opposition was almost fun. After nearly thirteen years of a daily "what's wrong with you, why can't you, why didn't you" hammering, after nearly thirteen years of having to take "brain-clenching" care in every syllable uttered until you learned to say nothing to avoid saying something, you could finally let loose and go after the government.

Being in opposition would be like shooting fish in a barrel, many Liberals believed. And the Conservatives were such an easy target. A political force-fit of Members of Parliament and their supporters who were still far more Progressive Conservative or Reform or Canadian Alliance than they were Conservative, they had in common only their hatred of Liberals and their desire for power. So many of Harper's members had become candidates because no one in their riding of any achievement or maturity wanted to run for a party that was not going to win any time soon. Some of them were almost kids who were candidates only to get their foot in the door for some time later when both they and their party were ready. Now they had won, and now this undistinguished lot had their hands on the levers of power. Some of them were going to have to be in the Cabinet. The Liberals couldn't wait.

Harper realized his government's distinct limitations: a bad start could confirm what the media and public were looking for and set in motion something from which the party might never recover. In the House, during Question Period, a prime minister customarily answers questions only from the other parties' leaders, about 20 per cent or fewer of the total questions asked. In the first weeks of Parliament, Harper rose to his feet to answer virtually every question. Outside the House, his members offered scripted, child-like answers. This was embarrassing both for Harper and for his party. Both the opposition members and the media made fun of them. Yet Harper knew that this self-imposed muzzling was far less embarrassing than what his unprepared ministers might say and what the opposition and media could make of that.

The Liberals, on the other hand, didn't understand that there was one simple answer that even the most inept Cabinet minister could give to even the most damaging question, and Cabinet ministers could give this response each time, question after question, for many weeks, months, and even years. Recalling the Liberals' years in office, it was an answer that began, "For thirteen years . . ." or alternatively, "For thirteen long years . . ." followed by whatever litany these ministers wanted to spew about any policy or action or inaction of the previous Liberal governments. And after thirteen long years, because everything does seem wrong, it was easy for the Conservatives to take this approach, and made easier still because they knew the public and the media were thinking the same. Each time the Conservatives gave their scripted answer, they also grew more confident in the rightness of their own story and offered it with more conviction each time they gave it. In Question Period, in their thirty-five-second questions, the Liberals threw their verbal haymakers; in their thirty-five-second answers, again and again the Conservatives bloodied the Liberals' noses with their jabs. When Harper, and later his ministers, decided they could push their scripts farther, they added a few other similarly magic words: "This new Conservative government," followed by "will" or "is committed to," words of intention that, given the government's new-ness, no one could disagree with. If said with excitement and energy, these words might even make a listener hopeful. The Liberals could not lay a glove on Harper and his ministers. To the Liberals' great frustration, what thirteen years in government had made into con-ventional thinking about them only continued to be the angle of the day in opposition. No matter the mis-deeds of Harper's government, every new wrongdoing was still all about the Liberals.

The Liberals were also in the middle of a leadership race. After his election defeat, Paul Martin had resigned and Bill Graham was appointed interim leader. Graham's job, like that of a substitute teacher, was to keep some order while the direction of the party was being deter-mined far from the House of Commons in the leader-ship race, the Liberal MPs lining up behind one of eleven candidates, their futures tied to them, listening to them and not to Graham. But a substitute teacher has to survive only the day; the leadership race took many months. To the Liberals, this race seemed a time where rediscovery would begin as the candidates laid out their priorities and debated one another. But the race proved nothing so ambitious. The front runner, Michael Ignatieff, was so far ahead that he focused on avoiding controversy. His nearest challenger, Bob Rae, realizing he couldn't make up such ground on his own, looked to lay traps for Ignatieff to undo himself. The others were compromise candidates at best, irrelevant to the race except perhaps in any manoeuvrings at the end.

The end was the leadership convention in Montreal. Although Ignatieff's support stalled, his supporters stayed with him. Rae received only some of that support on later ballots. Two candidates, Stéphane Dion and Gerard Kennedy, whose initial support had come largely because they were neither Ignatieff nor Rae, agreed that whoever finished lower on the ballot that forced one of them out of the race would throw his support to the survivor. Ignatieff and Rae had few others left in the hall willing to support them. Almost all of the "Anybody but Ignatieff" and "Anybody but Rae" delegates moved to Dion, and Dion won. Virtually no one had seen this coming. Those at home and those in the convention centre watched transfixed: it was politics at its most dramatic, and it was not what the Liberals needed.

At the time, the convention had seemed to be exactly what the Liberals needed: a large national audience, a great contest, a chance to introduce an unconventional new leader to the Canadian people, and, in contrast to the obvious weakness of those around Harper, a chance through the leadership candidates to show off the depth of the Liberal "bench." But the drama had been about picking a new leader and all the games and manoeuvrings involved with that. The convention had produced a new leader, but only a hint at the new direction in which the party might go. That new direction would be for later. But that never happened.

Almost immediately Dion began travelling the country. If Canadians had known him at all before, it was as a passionate believer in causes, in Canada as the father of the Clarity Act, in environmental circles as the minister of the environment and the chair of the 2005 United Nations Climate Change Conference in Montreal. To those who didn't know him, he looked and sounded like a French intellectual. Now he crisscrossed Canada as he had done during his leadership campaign, but this time under a different kind of scrutiny, as someone worthy of knowing and important to know. He talked with impressive conviction about his theory of the "three pillars" of a twenty-first-century global world. He connected the economy and social justice with the environment, so that every benefit and every cost are considered to foster intelligent and enlightened decision-making and to produce healthy and sustainable living. Little by little, this was how Dion would define himself for the Canadian people. He would present them with a stark choice: do you want as your prime minister someone who believes in politics that has a purpose, or someone for whom the purpose of politics is politics? For Dion, this would have been a fine strategy, if he was the only person setting the agenda.

Politics is a competitive sport, and your opponent has plans too. Harper decided to interrupt Dion's "definition tour" to define Dion himself. Harper launched attack ads that caricatured Dion's physical appearance and record, making him look nerdy and weak, each ad having as its tag line: "Stéphane Dion: not a leader." Many in the public and in the media denounced the ads: "disgusting" and "politics at its worst," they said. But Harper knew that a message dismissed is not necessarily a message forgotten. With these ads, he had made Dion's task far harder, for Dion would now need to undefine himself in order to define himself as something else.

Dion faced two large obstacles in defining himself. First, he did not have deep residual support in his own party. During the leadership race, he had been the first choice of only a small percentage of delegates. When he became party leader, Liberal supporters wanted him to succeed, of course, because they wanted their party to become the government again. But when Dion's early days as leader did not go well, these Liberal supporters reacted as new friends do, not old friends. Most of these new friends didn't jump out to oppose him, but most of them didn't jump in to defend him either. When Dion needed some wind at his back, the wind wasn't there.

Then there was Ignatieff and Rae and their support-ers. Ignatieff and Rae had taken their loss in Montreal badly. They had been nearly lifelong friends. Friends are friends except when there is one prize that both of them need and only one can have. Both were children of parents whose calling had been in the world of public service when public service and Canada had seemed the highest calling. Both men had been born to the lives they had set out to live. And both were going places, to any place they wanted to go because they were stars. They would determine their own futures. For many years those futures went in divergent direc-tions: Ignatieff, the liberal/Liberal academic, journalist, and writer, in England and the United States; Rae, the socialist/liberal New Democrat politician, Member of Parliament, Member of Provincial Parliament, premier of Ontario, then retired politician, lawyer, and engaged citizen, in Ottawa and Toronto. Then finally at almost the same moment, at an age when each faced the question of a final career, of what all the rest had been mere preparation for, their futures converged in a rush. Each realized his own life story had to end one way—with himself as prime minister. Both men had the same final chapter. With the twists and turns and deals of the Montreal convention, each of them realized that story was over.

Whatever else they or their supporters did or didn't do during Dion's time as leader, Ignatieff and Rae didn't have their heart in Dion's leadership. Once the Liberal Party, even with its divisions, had been too strong to lose. Now the Liberal Party needed everybody at their best to win, and it didn't have everybody.

Dion faced one more large obstacle. It is not easy to look good in opposition, especially as the Official Opposition leader. The government sets every agenda, and the Opposition party reacts. The media are interested in what the government does because it is the government; they aren't interested in what the Opposition says it would do because the Opposition can say anything and can do nothing. So the Opposition is asked to comment, and the placement of its comment in a story depends on how "interesting" that comment is, and "interesting" usually in the provocative, not substantive sense. The difficulty is that there are only so many ways the Opposition party can say that a government is "incompetent," "inept," and "irresponsible" and sound anything other than whiny, nagging, and boring. And chances are as party leader, in this case Dion, you got where you are because you had something of your own to say that others found worthy. Now all that you talk about are the government's priorities, which are not your own priorities, and you have to talk about them as if they are important, until you get fed up hearing your own voice.

Furthermore you can't carve out an identity for yourself as a party leader, or your party as a party, by being only "not this" or "not that," at least not in any way you would like. The government sets out its story, which is easy for a government to do because it has the resources. Then, with every position it takes on the hundreds of issues that arise, the government reinforces that story, and because it is the government and has a large bureaucracy to do its work, it has a ready-made position on almost anything, even if that position were to be wrong. If there is any coherent narrative in the country, it is the government's. For opposition parties, the situation is different. For the New Democrats and the Bloc, their well-defined ideologies, never tested and twisted by governing, provide them an easy, reliable position on every issue that arises. For the Liberals, is their position what it was when they were the government or something different? But they were the government years ago, and circumstances change. Besides, now out of power, the Liberals have the chance to rethink those positions and do them better this time. Politics, however, does not wait. During the early months of Dion's leadership, on even the most uncomplicated issues, the Liberals seemed frozen in place. They had no easy, automatic position on anything. Every issue created discussion, which turned into debate, which created division, and gave to Dion the look of confusion and indecision. Unless the public wants only to get rid of a government, being "not them" is not enough. But for the Liberals, becoming what they want to be, clearly and identifiably, had not been easy.

Some people, though not many, can be never-endingly negative and still sound strong; Dion wasn't one of them. Having to win over an audience he couldn't be sure of, he would speak faster, his voice pitching higher, making him look and sound like a little boy who couldn't get his way. With Dion sounding like someone who anyone would want to tune out, people tuned him out.

Dion is a person of purpose and substance. He hadn't gone into politics to get his name in the paper, or to pad his resumé, or to set himself up for a lucrative,

post-political future. In mid-career, rigorously recruited by Chrétien himself, he realized that what he
believed in most and what mattered to him most could
be best achieved in politics. As a Cabinet minister, he
had had some considerable achievements. But in opposition, he would have to bide his time. The conventional wisdom of politics says that a government is not
defeated by its opposition, a government defeats itself.
With all the actions a government has to take, and
with prying eyes everywhere, every day in power is ten
more nails in a government's coffin. This had happened
to Trudeau. This had happened to Mulroney. This had
happened to Chrétien and Martin. For an opposition
party, the strategy, then, is not to go out and win over
the public with a compelling agenda but to attack the
government, pounding into it an eleventh and twelfth
nail each day to make its downfall more certain. An opposition party is not the government. A government
governs, and opposition parties oppose. An opposition
party laying out its intentions takes the focus off the
government and makes the opposition party the target
instead. Besides, if an opposition party lays out its best
stuff, other parties will steal it. Tactics rule.

As the beneficiaries of this wisdom, even though the
Liberals needed to rediscover what would make them
proud and why they mattered, even though the public

had been saying in a loud, clear voice that they needed
to know what Dion and the Liberals stood for, even
though Dion did not like to attack Harper and play political games and was not good at either, even though he
liked to focus on and was at his best focusing on the
bigger purposes of the country, all this did not matter.
Month after month, Dion and the Liberals attacked
Harper, offering little about their intended direction
because conventional wisdom said that this was the
way to do it since, in memory, this strategy had won
the Liberals their majority in 1993, and because the
conventionally wise were still around in the shadows,
and who could argue with them?

The conventionally wise had forgotten one important word in their own conventional wisdom: "A government is not defeated by its opposition, a government defeats itself *ultimately*." After eleven years, then
after fifteen years, Trudeau, Turner, and the Liberals
had defeated themselves; after nine years, Mulroney
and Campbell and the Progressive Conservatives had
defeated themselves; after thirteen years, Chrétien
and Martin and the Liberals had defeated themselves.
Ultimately is the essential word. It takes a pile of grievances for a government to defeat itself. Harper had
been around less than two years; the public was not yet
ready to kick him out. For the Liberals to become the

government, they would have to win power themselves.

Meanwhile, during this period of political frenzy, on matters about transforming the global economy and Canada's need to adapt, about poverty and the widening gap between rich and poor and the societal implications of that, about climate change, about the role best played by Canada and most needed by the world for Canada to play, the Harper government was doing little or nothing, and the Liberal Opposition was saying little or nothing. Political insiders, party members, and political media were absorbed by the action. On television networks, stories of Harper, his government, or the Liberals often led the news. Among the public, few watched—and few cared.

Harper knew that even with all the misdoings and non-doings of the Liberals, he was only a small part of the way to his goal. Most weeks, the Conservatives were barely ahead in the polls, and Harper knew it was unlikely that he could win over many new supporters soon. The task for his government remained what it had always been, to weaken and demoralize the Liberals. What Harper was doing was not first of all about him, his party, his government, or even Canada, except perhaps for some hoped-for moment well into the future. He wasn't going to get many New Democrat voters to swing over and support him, nor would he convince many from the Bloc. His actions, as always, were directed at the Liberals. Harper wasn't going to win over the Liberals with some compelling vision that he had for Canada. His purpose was to elect and re-elect a not-Liberal government. And to do that, his plan was to get liberals to give up on the Liberals, not necessarily on liberalism, though he hoped that might happen some day too. Harper knew that most Canadians still believed that in a healthy, prosperous Canada, we needed our neighbours and our neighbours needed us, and that government has an important role to play. Harper needed to get these liberals to give up on the smug, divided, conviction-less Liberals. Governing would not achieve that, but campaigning might.

Even after four years in power, Harper still thinks and acts more like a party leader than a prime minis-ter. He has never understood that on January 23, 2006, when he was first elected prime minister, he became the leader of all 33 million Canadians. Not only the 5,374,071, or 36.3 per cent, of voting Canadians who supported his party, but the 9,434,088, or 63.7 per cent, who voted against him, and the nearly 20 million, by age or by choice, who didn't vote at all. Not just those who like him, but those who hate him, who never in their lives will vote for him. He is their prime minister too.

As prime minister of a minority government, Harper might have been expected to extend a conciliatory hand here and there to some party or another, to get their support to keep his government in power. Yet he hasn't done this. He knows that his best possible position, short of the complete disintegration of the Liberals, is having a minority government where the Liberals are too weak to win. This situation is even better than having a massive majority of his own. The New Democratic Party and Bloc will not form a government. His job is to keep the Liberals as his own punching bag. If the Liberals are too weak to win, he can have a minority but act as if he has a majority, making himself appear strong and tough, making the Liberals look pathetic and weak. Conversely, the Liberals, with the other opposition parties, have a majority but have to act as if they have a minority, not being able to bring Harper down and win, making themselves look weak, always blinking before Harper's stare, and always losing the day. To the Liberals, Harper is saying in effect, You have a choice. Support me or bring me down. Support me, no matter what legislative bill I present, no matter how egregious and unconscionable a policy I introduce, in fact, the more egregious and unconscionable, the better because then in your Liberal/liberal heart you can't support that bill or you'll break your own heart if you do, or else vote against the bill, force an election, which thirty-six days later you know you'll lose. That is your choice: seem to win now by voting against the bill, and bring the government down, and lose thirty-six days from now and lose every day after that because you know I will pass the bill anyway when I win, or seem to lose now by voting for it and not bring the government down, so you don't lose thirty-six days from now, but in doing so you lose your heart and soul and pride, so you will lose later. Which do you want, to lose or to lose? For Harper, life doesn't get any better than this.

Every contentious vote—the gun registry, anti-terrorism sunset clauses, the mission in Afghanistan—has always come down to the Liberals. Canadians have mixed feelings about the issues at stake in these votes, and Members of Parliament do too. But the New Democrats and Bloc vote ritually against the government. What does the timing of an election matter to them? They can't win. Government MPs will vote for the matter in question because they are the government. That leaves the Liberals. The Liberals reflect the mixed feelings of the public, which in part is the reason the Liberals have been the government for most of the last one hundred years. But with the Liberals' recent history of division, a divided vote makes the Liberals appear divided. With a new party leader looking to define himself, a divided vote appears to the media and to the public as a "failure of leadership." And with the Liberals' recent absence of purpose, a divided vote looks like the Liberals are still conviction-less and dis-unified. With no obvious new policy direction to define themselves, the Liberals, it seems, are only what they vote, and so every vote, even on small, insignificant issues, is preceded internally by great traumatic debate. The result is that over many excruciating months, sometimes the Liberals have voted for and sometimes they have voted against, and sometimes some members have voted and other members have been allowed to abstain or not be present at all, and sometimes some members decided on their own not to be there or to vote the way they wanted no matter what anybody said—and this lack of discipline has created ill will and further divided the already-divided party.

Members of Parliament, especially Liberal members, are independent. Many see their ridings as their own personal fiefdoms. Their name, after all, is the one on the election ballot, they won, and so they can do what-ever they feel they should do. When the party looks to vote a different way from the way they want to vote, many Members of Parliament more times than not cite local sentiment and say something to the effect of, "Well, I can't support that" (as in, "Why would you ever imagine I could?!"). "I only won by 200 [or 2,000 or 12,000] votes last time. I'd lose for sure this time." A few times, one single issue affects a riding or a province so significantly that for an MP there can be no other overriding national electoral concern. The proper determination of the issue will affect life in that riding or province far more than whichever party becomes the government. For the people of Newfoundland and Labrador, and Nova Scotia, the Atlantic Accord, which meant for those provinces much more money or much less money in offshore oil revenue and equalization depending on whether it passed, is one such example. But in almost every other case, whatever benefit a member might achieve by voting against his or her party on an issue would be far exceeded by the benefit received if that member's party were to become the government.

Many MPs assume that it is possible to have it both ways, voting local or voting party at their own personal discretion, to achieve their greatest personal benefit. It seems not to occur to them that much of their support is because of the Liberal logo next to their name on the ballot, and that a split vote, given the current state of the Liberals, will weaken their leader and the party's overall campaign, weakening greatly their own chances of winning in the next local election. Every party caucus likes to talk of itself as a "team," but every caucus acts at times in a very un-team-like way. When a party is winning, members do as they are told, even if it is not what they want to do. When a party is losing, it is everyone for his or her own lifeboat. The situation is similar to that before a hockey game, if after a coach has laid out the team's game plan, one player says, "Well, I can't do that. I'm a scorer. That's what I am and everybody knows it. I can't be a checker, even for this one game. I have a reputation; I have fans. They expect me to score. I can't let them down." So this player goes out and tries to score, and the team loses. In politics, some members vote the way they want in order to win locally on an issue, or so they think, and every-body, themselves included, loses a lot together.

Month after month during Stéphane Dion's time as Opposition leader, this was the experience of the Liberals. They tried one voting strategy, then another, then another—hoping for a tactical answer when the only answer was making themselves formidable enough as a party to be a credible threat to bring the govern-ment down and to win. But the Liberals were not strong enough, and with each vote becoming more tangled, more conflicted, and more divided, they grew more frustrated. Several times in their own minds they drew a line in the sand for themselves. If Harper pushes across that line again, they said to themselves, there is no way. In their own words, "That would be swallowing ourselves whole." They will accept his humiliation no longer, they said; they are going to bring Harper down. Then at the last moment, they would back off. It is easy to bring a government down. It is hard, thirty-six days later, to win an election. And they knew they could not win. As embarrassing and humiliating as their reversals were, far more embarrassing and humiliating and lasting far longer is losing. Month after month, the Liberals and Dion grew weaker. So month after month, Harper forced contentious votes and watched the fur fly. The situation was exactly what he was seeking.

There is an irony about majority and minority governments: with a minority government, in opposition, if you aren't ready to win, month after month you grow weaker; with a majority government, in opposition, if you aren't ready to win, month after month you grow stronger.

Then Dion, faced with a revolt in his own party and with a summer ahead that would only give time to his opponents, delivered what was in him to deliver. The Green Shift was an ambitious plan that in various ways would push carbon toward its proper cost, encourage other more benign sources of energy, generate new technologies and new directions for the economy, and produce additional revenue to meet social justice needs, including a rigorous fight against poverty. Here were Dion's "three pillars": the economy, social justice, and the environment. For politics and the political circumstances of the moment, however, the Green Shift was both too detailed and too slight, too different to understand easily and too hard to explain, too easy to sow confusion about, too easy to mock and, for Dion, too late. The public had stopped listening to him.

Although he had everything going his way, Harper could still not push his poll numbers into majority government range. The public did not like or trust him enough. The public still needed to see in him what it had already seen, only to see it differently; the public still hoped to see in Dion what it had not yet seen. The public wanted more time to decide, so Harper wouldn't give it more time. In September, he called an election.

Although the campaign had what seemed to be some turning-point moments, it was over before it began. Many non-"dyed in the wool" Liberals or Conservatives said during the campaign that what they wanted most was a "not–Stephen Harper" government. Because neither the Bloc nor New Democrats could win, that could only mean a Liberal government. Confronted with their own logic, however, many of these "soft" Liberals and "soft" Conservatives demurred. Although Stéphane Dion, most agreed, was an intelligent and honest man, he could not pass their most basic test: they couldn't see him as their prime minister.

For the Liberals, the election was a wipeout. Winning only 77 seats, the Liberals received only 26.3 per cent of the vote, their lowest total since Confederation. Perhaps even more significant was the non-partisan political story of the election. Only 59.1 per cent of eligible voters cast their ballots, the lowest percentage in Canadian history. The Conservatives, Liberals, New Democrats, and Bloc all received fewer votes than they had in 2006. Not interested in the choices it was given, not interested in the politics it saw, the public stayed home. No matter which party won, the public had lost.

On election day, in the polling booth, just as in 2006, imagine if Canadians had been offered a choice, not of candidates, but of the following scenario:

We still don't like Stephen Harper much, and we still aren't sure we trust him. On the whole, we still prefer the Liberals to the Conservatives, but after nearly thirteen years as government, they needed time out of power to re-find the best that is in them, and to find their energy and purpose again. So in 2006, we delivered that message, yet the Liberals didn't get it. Now we want to deliver the message again, but more forcefully. We don't want Harper to have a majority, and we still want the Liberals to be within striking distance for the next time: so we want Harper to have many more seats and the Liberals to have many fewer than before. We want the message to be so clearly on the wall for the Liberals that this time they can't miss it.

If Canadians, making their 13,834,294 individual decisions, had been given that choice, the great majority of them would have voted for it. On October 14, 2008, they again received what they wanted.

The great recession had begun; Ontario's manufacturing sector was being decimated; climate change discussions, which would culminate in Copenhagen more than one year later, were going nowhere. The focus of Ottawa was on the ups and downs of the Liberal Party, and on the manoeuvrings of Harper. The focus of most Canadians was everywhere else. It seemed to most Canadians that politics was supposed to be more than this and that more important matters were going on in the country and in the world that might change lives and change futures. It seemed to most Canadians that we were better than this. Some turned away; many wanted to scream.

OTTAWA III

Lessons not Learned

THERE HAD BEEN THREE elections in slightly more than four years. Harper was now undeniably in command, the Liberals were in even greater disarray, facing a new leadership race amid increased sourness and division. The economy was all that mattered. Politics would now shift to the back burner.

Only six weeks later, there was a fiscal update by the minister of finance, who told Canadians about the state of the economy given the global recession, laying out any immediate steps that needed to be taken in advance of a full budget two months later. The United States and United Kingdom had already announced significant government spending to stimulate their struggling economies and to save vulnerable jobs; France and Germany would do the same a few days later. In his own update, Finance Minister Jim Flaherty offered much less than what the urgency of the circumstances demanded, and opposition parties reacted harshly, saying that a two-month wait for the budget was too long. But it was another part of Flaherty's statement that triggered the ensuing visceral reaction. He announced the end of public subsidies to political parties. Until now, these subsidies had provided to parties a specific amount of money for each vote their candidates received in the previous election. In times like these, Flaherty explained, everyone needed to tighten their belts, political parties included.

A few years before, Prime Minister Jean Chrétien had pushed through legislation to eliminate large contributions to political parties from any one source. The maximum any individual could give was $5,000 a year; the maximum any company or union could give was $1,000 a year. It didn't matter how many candidates or parties a donor gave to, or in how many parts of the country, it didn't matter if that donor was the richest person or the poorest, Acme Plastering or the Royal Bank, the total from that one individual, company, or union could not exceed $5,000 or $1,000. Later, Harper had lowered those amounts even more, so that by November 27, 2008, the date of Flaherty's fiscal update, the maximum contribution allowed was $1,100 a year for individuals only; corporate and union contributions had been eliminated entirely.

Even though this election funding reform had been introduced by the Liberals, it had hurt the Liberals the most. With no funding limits, the Liberals had been able to receive large amounts from relatively few sources for their campaigns, and being the government most of the time, they did. All it took was a few "bag men" getting on the phone to make their "$100,000 calls." The Progressive Conservatives funded themselves this same way until conservative support fragmented in the 1993 election. The Progressive Conservatives, reduced to only two seats, were not going to be the government any time soon. Nor was the new Reform Party. To raise any money at all, the two conservative parties would need to attract it in much smaller amounts from a far wider array of willing supporters. So they adapted, changed their expectations and fundraising approaches, and did the best they could. The Liberals, with no reason to change, didn't change.

When election funding reform came in 2004, the conservative parties were ready; the Liberals were not. Even now, several years later, the Liberals were still gnashing their teeth about the difficulties of this "new" system, about how the old fundraising strategies didn't work any longer, all the time doing little to change themselves, as if they were still waiting for the "big boys" to leap back into action. The Conservatives, in Harper's "permanent campaign," week to week and minute to minute, have been permanently fundraising. As of December 2008, just after the fiscal update, the Conservatives had 112,184 donors; the Liberals, with far broader and greater traditional voter support, had only 30,890.

Then Flaherty made his announcement, and its effect was stunning. The Liberals, New Democrats, and Bloc should have adapted sooner to the fundraising changes; it was their own fault that they didn't. Yet Harper's and Flaherty's actions could only have been premeditated. The Conservatives, by virtue of receiving more votes than any other party in the 2008 election, had received the most money under the public subsidy provision, and with the elimination of this provision might lose the most in the future. But to the Conservatives, because of the success of their other fundraising, money raised through public subsidy mattered to them far less than to all the other parties. As a result, with the Conservatives eliminating the subsidy, over the next few elections and, with minority governments, maybe more, the Liberals, New Democrats, and Bloc would have much less money than the Conservatives to mount an election campaign, and would have a far harder time competing and potentially winning. With one seemingly innocuous blow, the Conservatives were dramatically reducing democratic choice. In politics, where nothing is breathtaking, this announcement was breathtaking. And what turned the stomach even more was that this announcement came in the midst of an economic crisis, which, so far as anyone knew, was the worst since the 1930s and might get worse still, where government was needed more than it had been needed in a long time, where every element of society needed to work together, trust one another, and focus on one thing: the economy. Then came this announcement, which was so utterly political, so utterly partisan, and so utterly non-democratic.

With the weakness of the Liberals, Harper knew he could get away with his scheme. "Support me or bring me down," he could taunt again, and the Liberals wouldn't dare bring him down. This would be one more humiliation for the Liberals, which would eat away at them until they screamed, "Enough! I'm not going to take this anymore," bring the government down, then get humiliated even more in an election.

But something different happened. The Liberals, New Democrats, and Bloc started talking. In the end, they agreed to a "coalition" between the Liberals and New Democrats whereby the prime minister would be Liberal, the great majority of Cabinet ministers would be Liberal, but there would be a few New Democrat

ministers too, and the Bloc would support this coalition on votes of non-confidence for a period of two
years. There were large problems in this arrangement.
No federalist party, it was said, could ever make a deal
with the Bloc, "the Separatists," and though the Bloc
was not a formal part of the coalition, a deal with the
Bloc would be necessary. Yet there was more, and still
worse. Under this arrangement, a Liberal would hold
the position of prime minister, which meant that the
Liberal leader, Stéphane Dion, whose party under his
direction less than two months before had been re-
soundingly rejected with only 26.3 per cent of the
vote and who had announced he would step down after
the Liberals had chosen a new leader at their leadership convention in May five months later, would be
prime minister.

Constitutionally, such a coalition was possible, even
if the Conservatives yelled loudly that this was nothing
more than a "coup" of the opposition parties. A government needs to show it has the confidence of the
House of Commons. Confidence means having the
support of the majority of its members in a vote that is
specifically a matter of confidence. A few days later,
such a vote could be held. The government would not
only lose the vote, but the opposition parties could
then present to the Governor General an alternative to

holding another election when one had so recently been held. The opposition parties could demonstrate to the Governor General that this "coalition" did have the confidence of the House because it had the support of the majority of its members. There had been coalitions before, though not federally, and there had been deals between parties that had allowed for a party with minority support to govern. In many Western democracies, these arrangements happened all the time.

To the majority of Canadians, however, this scenario, even if legal and possible, didn't seem right. There had been an election; Canadians had voted. It didn't matter that the Conservatives had received only 37 per cent of the vote; the Conservatives had won. They would be the government until they were voted out in some future election. Equally disturbing for the public was the great economic turmoil of this time. Bad stuff had happened; worse might be ahead. Canadians were counting on their government and needed the stability of what they knew. A coalition? A coalition supported by the Bloc? A prime minister people cannot see as their prime minister for five months until there is a new prime minister who might be anybody? Better the devil we know than the devil we don't, Canadians said.

There were only a few days until the non-confidence vote. The political parties and the political media were overcome by the panic, excitement, and fear of the moment. Whatever the implications, they were for tomorrow. That this was so "interesting," that was for today. This time Harper's "Support me or bring me down" wouldn't work. Harper went to Governor General Michäelle Jean to prorogue (shut down) Parliament before a vote could be held. The Governor General acceded, and Harper won a seven-week reprieve. But after his meeting with Jean, Harper looked shaken to his bones; his imperial manner had shrivelled away. He looked like a little boy who had been caught.

With almost no support remaining in his caucus and a critical time ahead, Dion was pushed into resigning immediately. The three-person leadership race that had developed between Michael Ignatieff, Bob Rae, and Dominic LeBlanc had quickly turned into a one-person race with Ignatieff far ahead. Liberals wanted more than anything to avoid more division, which a five-month Ignatieff-Rae showdown would generate. LeBlanc dropped out. After heated persuasion, so did Rae. Ignatieff became interim leader, subject to being confirmed at the Liberal convention in May.

Quickly, the panic, excitement, and fear of the political parties and political media subsided; the implications of such a coalition suddenly seemed like today's business, not tomorrow's. What had been so "interesting" didn't seem the point anymore, and Canadians rushed away from politics and toward their holidays. When Harper reappeared a few weeks later, his manner was back. Bolstered by the arguments of his supporters, and bolstered even more by his time alone to seethe and resent, he regained his unquestionable sense of rightness, made stronger now by a heightened edge of aggrievement.

Though officially only interim leader, Ignatieff was now the Liberal leader. He shared the public's discomfort with the coalition, and while not rejecting it formally, he didn't criss-cross the country to sell it as he would have needed to do to keep the coalition alive. Instead, for a month the coalition hung there, like a helium balloon little by little losing its lift, until sinking to the ground.

When Parliament un-prorogued in late January 2009, Finance Minister Jim Flaherty delivered his budget. This time the budget was far more in keeping with the economic urgency of the moment. Gone was any mention of the elimination of public election subsidies. Ignatieff told Harper that he would support the budget, though only on certain conditions. He would put the government, in Ignatieff's words, "on probation," setting out three general measures against which he needed the government to show progress and on which it would be graded—protecting the vulnerable, protecting the jobs of today, and creating the jobs of tomorrow. He also set out three dates on which report cards would be issued, the first two months later, the next before the summer, the last early in the fall, each date timed to allow for an election during a regular—not midsummer, not midwinter—Canadian election period, should Harper fail. Further, within days of each report card the Liberals would also have a Liberal Opposition Day on which they could bring a non-confidence motion to topple the government. Harper agreed, and the budget passed.

In those early days as Liberal leader, Ignatieff seemed remarkably comfortable. During Question Period, his questions were well thought out; they had a point; they were actual questions, not just partisan rants. Ignatieff appeared calm and purposeful in delivering them, undistracted by the hoots and hollers of government members or by the prime minister's occasional snipes. In television interviews, he was the same. Like a top performer in any field, Ignatieff seemed able to slow down time to his time. In his own mind, he had something worthy to say that his audience would want to hear, and so he kept going where he wanted to go, knowing his audience would go along with him, which they did.

When ten-year-old boys dream of being Sidney Crosby, they not only wear the Pittsburgh Penguin's number 87 on their backs, but they also think "Sidney Crosby," they feel and act "Sidney Crosby," they dream "Sidney Crosby." In their games—what would Sidney Crosby do if he had a breakaway, if the goalie was in this position or that? Would he go to his backhand? Would he "go 5-hole"? Last minute of the game, ahead by a goal, their goalie out, a faceoff in his own zone— what would he do? And between games, what would he eat? What would he wear? In all those interviews, what would he say? How would he say it? Those ten-year-olds don't want to be like him; they want to *be* him. So day after day, they are Sidney Crosby. For every game they play on the ice, they play fifty games in their heads. When they look up and see no one between themselves and the goalie, when they have that faceoff in their zone with a game on the line, they know what to do. They have done it hundreds of times before. And they do it, and we watch transfixed—he is only ten years old! How could he do that? Where did he learn?

When Michael Ignatieff was ten years old, his favourite player was Jean Béliveau. But when Ignatieff was ten years old, he didn't only dream of being Béliveau or even Rocket Richard or Gordie Howe as other boys did, he dreamed of being prime minister.

What would a prime minister say? How would he say it? Later when Ignatieff was a journalist and teacher, watching politicians in other parts of the world up close, what would that president or prime minister do? he wondered. So at age sixty-one, when Ignatieff stood in his place in the House of Commons for the first time as interim Leader of the Opposition, he had been there before, hundreds of times.

That adeptness continued through his early months. New hires were made; his fundraising staff seemed sharper. The leaks from Liberal caucus, so notorious in the past, stopped. Everything was more professional. During the previous two years, the Liberals had seemed always to be looking for the big play, the sudden policy masterstroke, the tactical tour de force at the right moment to bring the government down. With Ignatieff, there was a developing certainty and confidence that the Liberals could win the slow, substantial way, getting steadily, incrementally better all the time. And the public was noticing too. Canadians were feeling no great affection toward Ignatieff; it was at least too soon for that. But a respect was growing, the kind that comes with a subtle nod of the head, what Stéphane Dion could never quite achieve, which says, "Yes, he could be our prime minister." Ignatieff moved ahead in the polls.

Then Harper's attack ads hit. Crudely done, almost comic-like in form, they hit where attacks are supposed to hit: at the greatest vulnerability, where the greatest doubt, where the deepest unanswered question lies. With Dion, behind all his intellect and decency, the question had been, "Is he a leader?" Can he be a real prime minister? With Ignatieff, it was about all those years he had spent outside Canada. For more than thirty years, through nearly all of his professional life, Ignatieff had lived in England or the United States. Now that he was back in Canada, as the ads asserted, was he only "just visiting"? This was a question Ignatieff had surely been prepared for, yet he didn't seem prepared. At first, he tried to focus his response on the bully-centred nature of Harper, who had directed a character assassination of Dion. Now Harper was trying to do the same to him, and Canadians deplore such indecency, Ignatieff said. This strategy worked a little, and such ads did diminish Harper at least slightly among those in whom he was already greatly diminished. But the ads also diminished politics in general and all those who venture into it, bringing everybody down, leaving Harper, needing only to meet a lower standard, largely untouched. The attack ads worked for Harper in another way too, confirming in the minds of the public the utterly different world of politics and the need for a person like Harper. Nobody else is mean enough. After all, when you go to war, whom do you want on your side?

Ignatieff also tried to go on the offensive. He had lived outside Canada, but so had countless other Canadians. Like him, their careers had taken them there, or like millions of others, immigrants to Canada, they brought years and years of learning to Canada, just as he was now doing, making Canada even better. Is Harper saying that there are Canadians and there are *Canadians*, and that some Canadians are not as fully Canadian as others? Here, Ignatieff may have succeeded in seeding the ground for some future political nurturing. But among those neither confirmed supporters nor confirmed opponents of Harper, it is unlikely that many emerged from these attack ads with new confirmed feelings. It is likely that most emerged less able to forget that their deepest unanswered question about Ignatieff had still not been answered. "Why did he leave?"

Ignatieff might have said, as was certainly the case, that he carried "home" with him as he went "away," and it was away where he discovered the location of home, where what matters to him lies. Sometimes you do have to go away to know that. He might have said, as was certainly the case, that when he went away, he didn't realize how much he was taking Canada with him, that Canada was in him in the way he saw things, in his belief in the importance of government, and in the role we all play in the lives of one another. And he might have said that to understand home, you have to see and understand away. To know Canada, you have to know the world, not only to understand what all those millions of Canadians from the world have inside them that they have brought to Canada but to know where Canada fits into the world, why Canada matters, and what Canada can mean to the world in the future.

Ignatieff might have said, as surely he had the right to, why do you, the media, and the public focus only on me leaving? What about Harper staying, never going anywhere, never even leaving the shores of North America before he became leader of the Conservative Party in 2004? For the first forty-five years of his life! The answer is not that he was impoverished. He came from an upper-middle-class family, and he had lived an upper-middle-class life. Those of his generation "went travelling" as part of one of life's rites of passage. They were the Canadian "backpackers" of legend who displayed their flag for the world to see. They went away to discover and test themselves, to learn, to come back changed, with new energy, new appreciations, new understandings of Canada, and new reference points for a world in which they would be spending their futures.

How could Harper not have done this? Why does he have this need always for the familiar—in things, people, place, and thought—for fast and forever certainty and answer, always to be in the comfortable bosom of control? Why this monumental incuriosity? Why did he never leave?

And Ignatieff might have said, as he surely had the right to, what did Harper do during all those years himself? As Ignatieff was learning and achieving, what great deeds was Harper doing? What great thoughts was he sharing with the world? with Canadians? with Calgarians? with anybody?

What Ignatieff should have learned from the attack ads is that if you don't define yourself as what you want to be, someone else will define you as what they want you to be. This had happened to Dion, and Dion hadn't learned. It turned out that Ignatieff didn't learn either.

For Ignatieff, while the ads took some of the wind from his sails, they didn't capsize him as they had done Dion. It was what happened next that surprised him.

The first reporting period at the end of March had gone as easily for Harper and Ignatieff as both of them had needed it to. Neither wanted a confrontation so soon. It was then only two months into the "proba-tion" period, and not much information could yet be gathered to see if the Harper government's measures were being met. Nor did the media expect much. When the media asked the question they always asked, which can trigger the inflexible positions that can trigger the rest, "Are you going to bring down the government?" they received an answer they deemed reasonable for the moment, "This isn't the time." The next time would be different.

By mid-June, more time would have passed: more time for the Liberals to raise more money, to organize a campaign, to get their platform ready. There would be the momentum from Ignatieff's coronation at the Liberal convention in Vancouver, the dysfunction of the House, the attack ads. There would be the momentum of the by now five-year cycle of never-ending election, or rumoured election, or anticipated election where among the parties, and especially among the media, if not the public, there was sheer boredom for anything but the high anxiety of a possible election. Politics is a chicken game, and so the reporting of politics is often about the media standing between the parties, trash-talking both of them, then watching the feathers fly. At the next report card in June, there would be plenty of reasons to go or not to go, but all these other factors, piling higher each day, making a go far easier to explain and so far easier to do, would be the determinant. At moments like this, it is not about whether you go or not, it is that whatever you do, your reason is better than the other person's reason. The reason is not about doing right, it is about looking right doing right or wrong because that is what will seem right, and what seems right is what will win the day.

When the Liberals had been weak and Dion had been their leader, they decided that it was Dion who had made them weak. So a new leader was necessary. Ignatieff was strong. So when Ignatieff became leader, the Liberals would become strong. And, for a time, that seemed the case. But the Liberals weren't strong. The public kept saying to the Liberals in poll after poll, year after year: What are you about? Why do you matter? And year after year, the Liberals told the public what Harper was about, why Harper didn't matter, and why the public should not vote for him. And the public kept saying, To vote for you we need to know you, and the Liberals kept refusing to hear. By June, and after the attack ads, Harper realized that the Liberals were in no better position than they had been under Dion. So as the next report card approached, Harper got pushy again. You can grade me any way you want, Harper said, but you have the same choice you have always had: you can support me or you can bring me down.

On the deadline day for the second report card, Ignatieff announced to the media that after his negotiations with Harper, the latter had agreed to discuss what until then he had rejected: the potential for unemployed workers—after having worked a reduced number of hours—to be eligible for Employment Insurance benefits. Harper also agreed that the Liberals would have an Opposition Day a few days after Parliament resumed in late September. At that time, if the Liberals were not satisfied with the Employment Insurance resolution, they could introduce a non-confidence motion to bring down the government. Because of these concessions, Ignatieff said, the Liberals wouldn't force an election.

Ignatieff had the stronger case. The public didn't want an election; it wasn't the right moment to have an election. Yet in this game of political chicken, Harper was going to power straight ahead, no matter the consequences. Somebody had to decide that this was a stupid game and put an end to it. And Ignatieff did that: he prevented the election the public didn't want and the country didn't need. But in his media scrum, Ignatieff didn't sound like he believed his own message. His manner didn't shrivel away as Harper's had the previous December, yet Ignatieff fumbled. In the game of chicken, when Harper hit the gas, Ignatieff veered off. To the media, then to the public, that was the story.

For politics, the good thing about the summer is that nothing happens because the public isn't paying attention. For Ignatieff and the Liberals, the bad thing was that because nothing happens, nothing disturbs the last impression of the parliamentary year. Although Ignatieff had had a good first six months in 2009, this was now gone from memory. Ignatieff had blinked. With every week that passed during that summer, the implications of this political embarrassment grew. In the media and in the public, there was a quiet but audible buzz: Ignatieff is weak; he is just an academic; he stands for everything and stands for nothing. Ignatieff is another Dion.

Ignatieff and his advisers now had the summer to mull over what had gone wrong those final few days, and to set the plan for the fall. Events would happen fast. Little could be done the rest of June, then came Canada Day, then vacations, and then some long weekends. Suddenly it would be the national caucus meetings in Sudbury in early September. Then after Labour Day, when the public might start paying attention to politics again, the Liberals would do media ads. But the public and the media don't do much more than gather impressions about party leaders until they see them head to head in the same place at the same time. The Liberals would need Parliament to reopen before they could achieve much. But then during that first week of

Parliament in mid-September, Harper was going to Washington, then the next week was a parliamentary break week, then on September 28, a Liberal Opposition Day, a non-confidence vote, and the possibility of an election campaign beginning a few days later. The Liberals had so little time and so little opportunity to establish what they needed to establish. And election campaigns, even with party platforms, cannot establish what party leaders and parties are about. Election campaigns are too short, there is so much noise, so much "he said/she said," so much confusion over each party's program announcements—"Was that $3 million or $3 *billion*? Was that over one year, or ten?" If a party and party leader are depending on an election campaign to establish themselves, a campaign is too late.

Ignatieff's advisers also knew that as soon as they opened themselves up to the media, the first words out of the media's mouths wouldn't be a question but a challenge: "You're going to an election, right. I mean, you can't *not* go to an election. Harper got you into that chicken game in June and you backed off. You can't back off again." So what was Ignatieff's answer, one that he believed and one he thought the public would believe? The answer had to connect to a path to victory that was absolutely credible and possible now or at a different planned-for date a few months later. The answer would have to be ready no later than the first day of national caucus, September 1. The media would be there.

Ignatieff and his advisers needed to work on an answer for both options, to go or not to go, until they believed each answer equally. In circumstances such as this, a party almost always goes with its best-sounding answer, the one that seems most credible and deliverable to itself, even if the answer is the wrong one. During the summer, however, the core of Ignatieff's staff were in Ottawa, largely cut off from anyone else. There were no weekly caucus meetings—as there are during the rest of the year—for Liberal MPs to receive hints of Ignatieff's thinking and plans as they are developing, no chance for them to pass on what they were hearing as they knocked on doors in ridings all over the country. Together and isolated, and stung from what had happened in June, Ignatieff and his advisers built up and reinforced in one another the sense of rightness and confidence they needed. Yet the problem remained: the public didn't want an election. If Ignatieff's advisers had developed alternative options, if they had come up with the best case for both, they would have told him the following:

The majority of Canadians don't like Harper. A significant percentage of that majority admires him grudg-
ingly and doesn't dislike him enough to vote against

him. Together with those who support him, and given close to traditional and foreseeable levels of support for the Bloc, New Democratic Party, and the Green Party, this will still be enough for the Conservatives to win a minority government. Conventional wisdom says that opposition parties don't defeat governments; governments defeat themselves. If conventional wisdom is correct, we will lose.

To win now, we will need to run against conventional wisdom. The Conservatives won't lose; we will have to win. To get the support of Harper's lukewarm voters, those voters must find a reason to vote *for* us. We—you, the party leader, and the party—need to give Canadians that reason. And the polls, the media, and the "front steps" across the country say that we haven't done that yet.

Further, the great majority of Canadians do not want an election. But the great majority says that same thing before almost every prospective election. Then, when the election is called, each party blames the other parties for triggering it. Neither the media nor the public reach any clear conclusion to attribute their blame and, even if one party is implicated more than the others, no party pays an electoral price.

We have to develop a plan that you and all of us believe in. And no plan is a good plan unless it ends

with the right punchline—a Liberal government, minority or not, after the next election. A plan can sound
great, it can sound more doable, more exciting, more
of what we think a plan should be, but if that plan is
more likely to result in defeat than in victory, it is a
bad plan. Every plan, going to an election or not going
to an election, has to be judged equally against this
standard.

Plan A is for an election in the fall.

Why? We are much more ready than we have been at
least since 2006. We have more money, we are better
organized, we have a strong, credible leader. No matter
what the Harper government does, whether it has a
good month or bad, the public has not warmed to it.
The Conservatives are in free-fall in Quebec. Giving
Harper more time gives the public more time to grow
more comfortable with him. More time allows him to
get a bounce from the end of the recession, and from
the afterglow of what will surely be a hugely successful
Olympics in February.

But even if all this wasn't true, we can't keep threatening and then not go to an election. Threatening then
backing off makes you look weak and reinforces all the
messages they are hitting you with—an "academic," a
"here today, gone tomorrow" visitor. And that chicken
game Harper loves to play, we can't let that happen

again. To show that you are serious and that we are serious, we have to go in the fall.

Further, we will also have some momentum—our national caucus in Sudbury; your visit to China; our ads; the opening of Parliament. Again, and most crucially, we can keep pointing out Harper's flaws. But more than this, we have a responsibility. We are the Opposition. If they are this bad, how can we justify keeping them in power? If we cannot answer that question, we have to go to an election.

Plan B is for no election in the fall.

Why? We are less likely to win. For all the reasons set out above, the public doesn't dislike Harper enough, and they don't like us enough, and there is not enough time or opportunity between now and September 28 to change that. Further, the public doesn't want an election, and this time it *really* doesn't want an election. To the public, we have already had so many elections in the last few years. The public looks at the polls and sees another minority government ahead, which only means another election a few months after that, and all the public has seen from the last few minority governments is nastiness, dysfunction, never-stop politics, and the absence of any proper governing. The public doesn't think that minority governments work; it sees the Conservatives and what they are, but it doesn't see the Liberals offering anything different of their own. People say again and again, "We do not see any real differences between the parties." They see only politics, and to them everybody's politics looks the same. So to them, "minority Liberal" or "minority Conservative," what does it matter? It is only the "minority" or the "majority" of a government that makes the difference. Besides, these are tough economic times. Most Canadians have never in their lives needed their government more than they do now. If there is going to be another minority government, if minority governments don't work, if there is no real difference between the parties, why spend $300 million or $400 million on an election we cannot afford? And if all this is true, Canadians are saying, if you, the Liberals, do bring on an election, you must think you matter more than we do. To us, the public, elections are about *you*. Governing is about *us*. Now is a time about us. If you make it about you, if you force an election, we, the public, will be more than mad. We will resent you. Given these sentiments, if, as Liberals, we trigger an election, Canadians may punish us.

But if the answer to an election now is "no," how and when do we make it "yes"?

We begin by playing our game, not Harper's. As prime minister of a minority government with three opposition parties and only one that can defeat him, Harper is in the driver's seat and he knows it. The Bloc and New Democrats will always vote against him because they have nothing to lose. He knows the only party between Canadians and another election is us. He knows that Canadians don't hate him and don't love us. He knows he can approach Parliament on any matter at any time with the same ultimatum—support me or bring me down. And he can do that until the public hates him or until the public comes to like us more. The public hating him enough—that is in his hands; the public liking us enough—that is in ours.

Harper's game is politics; he loves it and he is good at it. Your game is politics too, but with some bigger purpose: prosperity and fairness at home and responsibility to the larger world beyond our borders. Your game is substance, and a style that emerges out of that substance. You are serious, and people expect serious from you. People expect games from Harper. Play your game—purpose and seriousness—and you will win. Play his, and he will.

It takes time to establish all this in the public's mind and the media's mind. So we tell the public that there will be no election because this is no time for an election. Because the public says it still doesn't know what we stand for, we tell them that we won't wait for a campaign but will spend the next months setting out for them what a Michael Ignatieff and a Liberal government would be.

Finally, to answer that most basic question, If the Conservatives are so bad, how can I justify keeping these guys in power? The answer is by understanding that this is not the question. The question is: "How can I get these guys *out* of power?" Bringing them down is easy; getting them out thirty-six days later, that is the hard part.

So, is it Plan A or Plan B?

In August 2009, Ignatieff's advisers might have laid out his options this way, then concluded:

Plan A offers an easier, more instinctive, and, at first, more obvious story. Plan B takes longer to accomplish, seems more complicated and uncertain of result, and offers the greater likelihood of short-term pain. But the best plan is not the one easiest to implement; it is the one most likely to succeed. Which plan can win?

Plan A is all about story, not punchline. Plan B demands a more challenging story but comes with the right punchline. Real pain comes not in the challenge of delivery, it comes in the losing. Plan A, which seems so pain-free in the beginning, is pain-full in the end.

Plan B offers the much greater prospect of winning and winning with an excitement and purpose that a government needs. Plan A is playing their game. Plan B is playing ours.

Plan A is the path Ignatieff and his advisers followed.

Ignatieff had seemed so comfortable and composed, so on top of everything right from the day he became Liberal leader. From his first boyhood imaginings, he had put himself inside the skin of prime ministers and presidents, living out their experiences with them, deciding for himself what he would have done, how he would have looked and sounded in their stead. He arrived into his new role fifty years experienced. But what were not in his boyhood fantasies, or much in his adult observings, were the tactics and manoeuvrings that make politics function. Here, he was not experienced. Here, he was not confident and comfortable. So he did what any smart person would do, he surrounded himself with people who knew that side of the game. Trudeau had had his Jim Coutts, Chrétien his Eddie Goldenberg, Ignatieff would have his own tactical mastermind. And that person, of course, would apply the conventional wisdom learned and earned in so many successful Liberal campaigns over so many years. Governments are not defeated by their opposition, they defeat themselves. Parties don't tell the public what they intend to do, other parties will steal their message. The public never wants an election. The Great Wall of China had worked, so the Maginot Line would work too. These tacticians had won before, they were Liberals. What right had he not to listen to them? He had yet to learn that depending on the circumstances, substance can be tactics too. He had yet to learn that a strategy based on the Liberals losing for eight years until the public grows tired of the Conservatives and kicks them out, then to win, is not a strategy that requires political genius.

Ignatieff had given up one other essential element in his years outside Canada, though that was not clear, perhaps even to him, until June and after. He had been back in Canada regularly during this time. He had been in many more places and had experienced them more fully than Harper ever had. He is not a true academic as Dion is. Dion's way was to search for clues outside himself, then to look inside himself, stretching, twisting, and testing ideas, and searching inside for his answers. "Absent-minded professors" appear absent because, immersed in their own inner worlds, they are often absent from the bigger world. But Ignatieff was more a journalist, more an observer than an academic. His way is to get up close to people and situations to see what is happening, then to retreat to his computer screen to try to make sense of what he has seen, and to apply an academic's framework and context to that. The closer he gets to something, the better he understands it, the more confident he is in expressing himself, and the more persuasive he is. At this critical moment, when the Liberal Party and Canadians needed some compelling new direction, Ignatieff was more confident of his understandings of the world than of Canada.

On September 1, 2009, Liberal parliamentarians opened their national caucus in Sudbury with individual regional meetings, one each for Atlantic Canada, Quebec, Ontario, and the West and North. They had the chance to talk about what they wanted to talk about, and most talked about the next election. The members then moved to a full national caucus meeting. The chairs of each regional group reported on their sessions, much of which related to the possible election. Then comments were made from the floor. First a scattering of members, then one after another, talked about the election. Members who had never agreed with one another before agreed this time. They had all heard the same thing all summer—there must be no election. After a brief break, Ignatieff came into the room and, with the media invited, gave a rousing political speech—Harper's time has run out, he said. We will no longer support this government. For the Liberal caucus, it was a *Saturday Night Live* Gilda Radner/Emily Litella moment—"Never mind."

With the Liberals' intentions expressed, the media and the public suddenly flipped over their "gone for the summer" signs and were open for business. The Liberals now had a month to make their case. But the public was not interested; they didn't want another election. They turned on Ignatieff. They had turned on Dion before, but this was worse. Dion was easier to dismiss but harder to pick on; in his shy, awkward way, he was almost likeable. With Ignatieff, if someone didn't like him, they wanted to hurt him. The Liberals' poll numbers fell dramatically. The public had been gentle in voting out the Liberals in 2006; they had been increasingly impatient in 2008, now they were getting mad: "You think 77 seats is low? How does 40 sound?" Looking lost, Ignatieff tried to make fun of his situation. To every ritual "How are you?" asked of him, he seemed compelled to answer truthfully, wry smile and all. But self-deprecation was not in his makeup.

The Liberals had no other way out. Ignatieff told the media that the public doesn't want an election. They want an alternative to the Harper government, and it was his task to build and provide one. The

Liberals' "lose for eight years until they lose" strategy was not good enough.

As Ignatieff tried to bring greater policy focus to his speeches around the country, the Montreal Conference became more important to him. He had raised the idea before he became leader. The party needed to be transformed. After the long Liberal reign of Mackenzie King and Louis St. Laurent, with Progressive Conservative Prime Minister John Diefenbaker in power, Liberal Opposition Leader Lester B. Pearson had convened the Kingston Conference. Twenty-one years of nearly uninterrupted Liberal governments followed. With Progressive Conservative Prime Minister Brian Mulroney in office, Liberal Opposition Leader Jean Chrétien convened the Aylmer Conference. Thirteen years of Liberal governments followed. There are not many people still around who had been at one conference or the other; many fewer remember what they had talked about. There had also been other conferences that had gone unremembered. But that was not the point. These two conferences had passed into legend. In memory, they seemed the serious and proper step to take for a party that was serious and ambitious. And each time the Liberals held a conference, Liberal fortunes had turned around. Symbols and turning points matter. When the Liberals needed to rediscover themselves, they had come together. They would do it again.

With its new significance, the conference was moved from January to March 2010 to give it additional time for preparation. Parliament recessed in mid-December for its scheduled return on January 25. Then came Harper's phone call to the Governor General on December 30.

Harper asked the Governor General to prorogue Parliament until March 3, and the Governor General acceded. The prime minister said that the additional time was necessary to recalibrate his government's approach to the economy. The Liberals said it was because the prime minister wanted to shut down parliamentary inquiries into the Afghan detainee issue. Prorogation is constitutional. Harper and most other prime ministers, including Chrétien, had used it before. The question was: in this situation, did it *seem* right? Could the Conservatives make it seem to the media and to non-committed voters that prorogation was minor enough to pass from view within days and mostly to stay there? Or could the Liberals make prorogation seem like something fundamental to add to the ever-growing pile of impressions—power-hungry, controlling, dangerous, dictatorial, vindictive—that the Liberals hoped to attach to Harper? At first, it seemed that this second prorogation would end up like every other large gaff Harper had made, as another potential source of Conservative weakness, though more likely as a show-case for the humiliating weakness of the Liberals—support me or bring me down. As much as Harper's actions helped the Liberals who were looking for help from any direction, prorogation was also a distraction for Liberals who needed most to address their own problems. For Liberals, it was all too irresistible—"Stephen Harper: Going Pro-rogue." The story could be about Harper again.

For a few weeks in the media and on the streets, the focus was all on Harper. *Prorogation*, a word few Canadians had known, a word that would need translation into daily English to be understood, became part of the common parlance, and everybody knew what it meant because everyone could relate it to their own lives. "Sorry, world, I know I'm supposed get up and go to work [take out the garbage/do my homework/back-check], but I don't want to, and you can't make me. I prorogue!" Sanctioned by the Constitution, upheld by the Governor General, prorogation was magic, and no matter what you prorogued from and didn't do, you got paid just the same. Neither the Conservative nor the Liberal spinners could control its message. The public determined that message for themselves. In the next polls, Harper's support dropped significantly; Liberal support was almost unchanged.

Prorogation had put the focus on Harper without the Liberals having to try to put the focus on Harper themselves. It gave the Liberals the chance to put the focus where they needed it to be, on defining their directions for the country; it was an almost unique opportunity. Parliament was shut down. This was not summertime where everyone, including the media, is on vacation and nobody wants anything to do with politics. This was late January and all of February, prime political attention time. The national media is in Ottawa. Newspapers still had to be sold, television screens still had to be watched. Journalists had time and space they needed to fill and no government in front of them to fill them. With Harper proroguing Parliament, there was only one place in the country that Harper and his Members of Parliament could not go—Ottawa. There was only one place in the country the Liberals wouldn't have to compete with the government for attention— Ottawa. The media don't like traipsing around the country sniffing after stories that aren't stories. If they must write non-stories, better to do that from home. The Liberals would need to act like good partners. They would need to provide the media each day with at least an excuse of a story. The story's details would not matter. In essence, each story would be about Harper shutting down Parliament when there was important work to do, and the Liberals were there, in Ottawa, on the job, doing what a proper government did, focusing on the important issues the country is facing—the economy, employment, poverty, public health, accountability—and doing so publicly in forums involving the most informed people in the country in front of the media and the public, in a manner that was serious, rigorous, and purposeful. In other words, during prorogation, the Liberals imagined they would do everything they believed the Harper government wasn't doing.

The media would be skeptical at first. They would see the Liberals' actions as a stunt, the Liberals merely substituting one form of objectionable politics for another. But if the Liberals day after day treated what they were doing as more important than they are themselves, slowly the media might treat them and their forums seriously too. The story for the Liberals was not about getting headlines; it was about earning the public's respect. The Liberals needed an angle-changer, and these forums gave them a chance.

Now with an audience, the Liberals needed something to say that was not simply about Harper. These forums were to provide the advice of informed people and not an outline of the Liberals' platform. Still the forums needed to suggest the directions the Liberals wanted to go and the spirit with which they intended to get there. But every time the Liberals made any vision, direction, or aspiration the focus, Harper made money the focus. He wanted the public to know that no discussion, no idle talk even, was about poverty or transforming the economy, it was about taxes. It was about Liberals jamming their hands into your pockets again. In this time of high deficit and diminished capacity in the federal government to act, Ignatieff seemed paralyzed.

Harper doesn't see the value in government. Government, he believes, should offer fewer services, and Canadians should get their money back, in the form of lower taxes, from the services no longer provided. The federal government should do what the federal government has the constitutional responsibility to do—foreign affairs, defence, immigration, criminal law, Aboriginal affairs, taxation, banking, unemployment insurance, trade and commerce, and little else. In 1867, Canada was only Quebec, Ontario, New Brunswick, and Nova Scotia, and no one in 1867 imagined an education system, let alone one intended to educate every young person to graduation from high school and most to college or university. As for health care, in 1867 families took care of their own at home with only a smattering of family doctors and hospitals paid for by churches or charities or the wealthy. In 1867, the most important powers had to do with the national economy, the collection of taxes, the defence of the realm, foreign affairs and international trade, powers given to the federal government.

Times have changed, and new needs have superseded old ones. The federal government, under successive Liberal and Progressive Conservative governments, has used the power of its purse to push into areas of provincial jurisdiction it saw as national priorities—health care, infrastructure, post-secondary education. Harper has worked to reverse this, retaining the federal government's taxing power even while reducing taxes, continuing the money transfers to the provinces but without earmarking the purposes for these transfers, allowing the provinces to spend the money in whatever way they choose. The result is a federal government that has less money looking to do fewer things, with most of its $280.5 billion budget already spoken for before any new priorities are identified: $37 billion is transferred to the provinces for health care, other social programs, and equalization; another $37 billion is for pension and other benefits for the elderly; $31 billion is to pay off debt; $23 billion for employment insurance, $21 billion for defence; $7 billion for Indian Affairs and

Northern Development. In a time of Afghanistan, with lives lost and thousands more putting themselves in harm's way, you can't cut the defence budget. You can't cut health-care transfers to the provinces, or equalization transfers or pensions. Add to these expenditures the general operating costs of government and not much is left for everything else. And add to that the now public mantra that taxes can never be raised and must only be cut, and that a budget must be in balance, and add to that a recession-driven $56 billion deficit that will decrease naturally as the economy improves, but not entirely. What can any prime minister do? Recognize that the capacity to learn is our only security and only opportunity for the future and invest in early learning and child care, post-secondary education, literacy, training, research, and new technologies? We can't afford it. Commit to a fight against poverty, to a fight for equity for Aboriginal peoples, for women, for people with disabilities? We can't afford it. Enhance the health, not just health care, of Canadians, to fight obesity and diabetes? We can't afford it. Raise taxes? We can't do it.

Harper is like a school headmaster with a cane. As soon as a student dares open his or her mouth with a thought, an idea, let alone a hope or a dream that has nothing to do with lower taxes, Harper brings that cane down—*wham!*—right across the knuckles. He has created a political box, and this is exactly what he intended to do. He has taken away money from the federal government; he has scorched the political earth on anything but tax cuts. He has made the thought of anything else mockable and outrageous. Minority government or majority government, it doesn't matter. Conservative government or Liberal government, it doesn't matter. There is no money. You can't spend what you don't have. You can't be what you don't have the capacity to be. You are what you have. With no money, everybody is the same. Harper has left the Liberals little room to be anything other than Conservatives. And while the Conservatives like being Conservatives and are proud of being Conservatives, the Liberals are lousy Conservatives and hate being Conservatives. And if the Liberals cannot make themselves proud of what they are, why would the public listen to them?

Harper has been counting on two basic understandings. He doesn't believe that the Liberals are liberals. He thinks they are intellectual and moral dilettantes. They believe in equity and fairness, but when faced with the option of equity and fairness and having to raise taxes in order to achieve that, Liberals will grumble, be sad, and then cut and run. For Harper, the recession makes the test for the Liberals even harder and sweeter. By offering the Liberals even less fiscal room, the recession further separates the believers and the real believers. To Harper, real liberals survive a recession; Liberals do not. Second, Harper doesn't believe that Canadians are generous. He thinks Canadians are like Liberals. They are hopers and dreamers, they want fairness and equity, but if they have to spend more in taxes to pay for fairness and equity, they will cut and run too.

Harper has been calling Ignatieff's bluff. Do you have a vision for this country? he wonders of Ignatieff. Because if you don't, if you don't have a story to lay out for Canadians of what they are and what they can be, a compelling, exciting, transforming story, then politics *will* be all about cutting taxes. Because nothing else you say will have a chance, and every time you open your mouth and talk about something that sounds like a vision, I will interrupt you with shouts and ads that tear you down—"just visiting"—and tear down everything you say—"just the 'tax-and-spend' Liberals again"—so that your vision will sound like nothing more than interrupted pieces, with no build, no momentum, no excitement, and no chance. Harper has been calling Ignatieff's bluff because he does not think Ignatieff has a vision that he believes in, and because he doesn't, Harper doesn't think Ignatieff will have the guts to call the bluff of Canadians. As Canadians, as human beings, we all have our good and bad sides. Harper believes that in a battle between our selfish selves and our unselfish selves, our selfish selves will win.

Harper is saying to Ignatieff and the Liberals, If you act like liberals, the public will kill you, and I will win. Or if you do not act like liberals, you will kill each other, and I will win.

George W. Bush made Obama possible; Harper is now making a great liberal possible because he doesn't believe there is one around.

OTTAWA IV
Politics and Story

PARLIAMENT HILL IS ALL POLITICS, even when it doesn't seem to be. Politics turns what is not politics into politics on Parliament Hill, for party leaders and strategists, for staffers and media. The issue is never about only climate change or child care; it is how a party can frame its message about climate change or child care, whether accurately or not, to have it understood by the media and public, whether fairly or not, so that its understanding becomes the public's understanding, so it can "own" the issue. Then it can demonize the other parties and their messages, most particularly their party leaders and the prime minister. When the Liberals are the government, the Liberals are the only target for all the other parties. When the Conservatives are the government, the Conservatives are the principal target, but the Liberals are also a target because the New Democratic Party and the Bloc compete with the

Liberals for similar philosophical (New Democrat) and geographical (Bloc) ground. If the give-and-take of politics is your love, Parliament Hill is your place. If it is not, Parliament Hill is de-energizing and demoralizing, where people imagine the worst, see the worst, and bring out the worst. It is a place that Members of Parliament need to get away from as often as they can, to rediscover the country, to rediscover why they are doing what they are doing.

Outside Parliament Hill, people are living their lives. They don't have the luxury of being cynical. Life is tough enough; they have to get on with all of life's demands. They have to seek the best and find the best. As a Member of Parliament, knock on any door anywhere in the country, work through the first awkward moments, and what you hear is hope, and what you see is try. You see this especially in small towns. In a small town, to build a park or a seniors' home or to put on a community dinner, the Rotary or Kiwanis, the churches, big local companies and small, government agencies and government officials, municipal, provincial and federal, everybody is needed. The pride and satisfaction in their efforts are obvious. For the politician arriving from Ottawa, having made two connecting flights with a two-hour layover between them, having driven the last hundred kilometres to get there and facing the same experience in the reverse direction a few hours later, you arrive with much less energy, and you leave with much more. The problem for the political media, which becomes a problem for politics and for the public, is that the media don't have the same opportunity to escape, to see what is not cynical.

To most Canadians, politics is games, trivial, inane games played by modestly talented people who are drawn as if powerless to the spotlight and who think that what they do is more important than it is. These people are at the helm of an instrument—government (politics, to most, being the personification of government)—so massive and lumbering that nothing happens unless it happens slowly. This government operates only at great cost to the taxpayer, whose money, without which the government could not exist, disappears without obvious trace or effect, and which would otherwise remain in the taxpayers' own pockets for them to do in smaller, tangible ways those things that matter to them and what are of their own choosing. Politics is not the art of making the possible possible. More often politics is the black art of—interrupting, intruding, tearing down—making the possible impossible. Yet, to most Canadians, politics is also something that should be respected; it should be a source of confidence and comfort. Everybody needs help at some moment in their lives. If we are lucky, that help will come from a parent or teacher, coach or friend, somebody who sees something worthwhile in us, who puts in extra time with us, a word of encouragement, advice, without which we aren't sure how our life would have turned out. Everybody needs a chance. Even the rich who have been rich all their lives at some moment need a chance too, in order to develop a new product, or to break into a new market, or to feel the full satisfaction and fulfillment they seek.

For those who aren't rich and for those who are poor, who didn't catch the eye of a parent or teacher, coach or friend, who didn't get the same help or have the same chance or who didn't give themselves the full chance they needed, what do they do? Where do they go? For them, for everybody at some moment, government matters; government is their last imaginable hope. And most Canadians make no distinction between federal, provincial, and municipal governments, instead thinking of them collectively as "the government." As Canadians, they paid for "the government" with their taxes. When they have a problem, whether it is garbage pickup or inaction on Darfur, they expect "the government" to transform itself into whatever "the government" needs to be to fix it. If "the government" doesn't, "It's just politics," they say, angrily, or defeatedly.

For most Canadians, the ineptitude of politics is not even the worst part. It is the blatantness of politics. If politics/government would allow itself sometimes to be part of the background like everyone and everything else, that would be fine. Instead—all the staged realities, the ribbon cuttings, the big ceremonial cheques, the shouted, over-the-top words, everything insistently bigger than life—it is when politics shoves its existence down the throats of everyone else that the public recoils. And the worst of the worst is Question Period.

Question Period should be one of our best democratic instruments. It offers forty-five minutes—each day that Parliament is in session—for the government to be held to account by critics from opposition parties in front of media and, by television, in front of the Canadian people. The questions are not submitted to the government in advance. No question can be longer than thirty-five seconds, and no answer can be longer than thirty-five seconds. After thirty-five seconds, the Speaker stands up, one of his staff pushes a button, and the microphones go dead. But most often the questions are not questions. They are sometimes outrageous assertions that attack the government for most of that thirty-five seconds, then, so as to be in proper form, with a quick question tacked on at the end. Most often, too, the answers aren't answers. They are also sometimes outrageous assertions that attack the opposition or sell the government. In a story, possibly apocryphal, associated with former Liberal deputy prime minister Herb Gray, after an exasperated opposition member claimed that Gray had not answered his question, Gray is supposed to have said, "This is 'Question Period.' They don't call it 'Answer Period.'" Nor does any "answer" need to be true. It is not up to the Speaker to determine truth. It is also not possible to call anyone who has lied a "liar." That is "unparliamentary language." Members of Parliament are "honourable members," and by definition honourable members do not lie. So an honourable member can use what he or she is by definition as a shield to hide behind to do what by definition he or she cannot do. And every prime minister knows that if you give the media something new every day, most have neither the interest nor the time to check into what happened yesterday. For the media, Question Period and the scrums it generates afterwards are perfect. The media can sit up in the seats at one end of the House and watch everything play out before them. Their story is all there—character, conflict, bizarre twists and turns, who wins and who loses, who's hot and who's not, which they can report on like last night's game. Then a new day, old day begins all over again.

For political parties, Question Period is approached like a team sport. Every question that shakes the prime minister or a minister, every answer that shakes an opposition leader or one of its members, is good for the team. Every question or every answer that fails lets your team down. And every question and every answer also brings cheers or jeers from the spectators—the other members—who fill the House. For opposition parties, who stew in the deep shadows of the government month after month, Question Period is a chance to remind their constituents that they still exist. It is a device, little by little, to destroy the reputation of the government and the prime minister. As much as it is to hold the government to account, Question Period is for opposition morale.

Every member wears an earpiece: for some, it is to hear the translation into French or English; for all, it is to hear the question or the answer above the din of the House. Against such noise, it is normal to shout to be heard, yet with an earpiece and with microphones that pick up the voices for transcription and for television, it is not necessary. In fact, those watching the seconds-long clip from Question Period at home on the late-night news, the clip edited to the context of the journalist's story and not necessarily to the events of Question Period itself, wonder, Why are these people shouting?

Why are they all clapping at something that seems un-important? Why are they all laughing at something that is not funny? For politicians and for politics, Question Period is perfect madness, something wilfully done that could be wilfully undone, showing every member at his and her worst.

In the course of a year, it is possible that a citizen might attend an event at which their local member is present. It is possible during an election campaign that the local member might knock on their door. It is more likely, however, that in the course of a year the closest exposure a citizen will get to their local Member of Parliament will be in a clip from Question Period.

Voter turnout in federal elections is down. In 2006, it was 64.7 per cent; in 2008, 59.1 per cent. In 1984, it was 75.3 per cent. In the fifteen elections in the forty-three years from the end of the Second World War to 1988, only twice was voter turnout less than 70 per cent. For those under thirty, voter turnout is much worse. For those who do vote, many do so only out of a feeling of personal obligation; they are citizens of a democracy. They vote because of a compelling belief not in one party or one candidate or another, but in their precious duty as citizens to vote. A question often asked is why more people, and why more young people, don't vote? Given their limited connection with politics, given what they see on television, the more pertinent question is why *would* they vote?

After every election and after every embarrassing voter turnout, there is a flurry of articles about what should be done: mandatory voting, a lower voting age, fixed dates for elections, proportional representation, an elected Senate, more public funding to open politics to more people of different backgrounds and circumstances, more women candidates, a more civil tone to Parliament, and more civics programs in our schools. Yet even if all these actions were taken, politics would not change much. We are looking in the wrong place for the answer to our problem, hoping to find the answer where we wish it to be. We are imagining this absence of interest in voting as a technical problem that has a technical solution. But politics is only an instrument. Politics is what political parties employ to do what they decide should be done. But politics is only worthy if the purpose of that politics is worthy. Our problem is not politics; our problem is *this* politics.

This politics happens when, as Members of Parliament and governments, we don't believe we can do what we know we must do—reduce poverty, reverse climate change, transform our carbon economy. This politics happens when, as members and citizens, we don't believe we are smart or committed or generous enough to succeed. To take on these issues costs money, tax-payer money; to take on these issues takes time and comes with no certainty of success. And if sometimes we think we are smart, committed, or generous enough, we are absolutely not certain about our neighbour and our neighbour's neighbour. Big tasks need everybody. Do we honestly believe that faced with a choice, our neighbour and our neighbour's neighbour will choose anything other than lower taxes from their government? When the crunch comes, those neighbours will turn away and never look back. They will vilify the prime minister for not doing what they don't have the will to do themselves, so they vilify themselves. The media will laugh. For anyone who is serious about taking on these big tasks, it is political suicide. To believe anything else is to be naive; to get others to believe is a fraud. But not to believe doesn't work. This politics happens when it doesn't seem there is anything bigger to believe in. We cannot fix politics by focusing on politics.

Harper's prorogation of Parliament in January and February 2010 brought surprising reactions. The public didn't shrug off prorogation as if it were nothing. Many people were angry and stayed angry for weeks, just as they had been with Ignatieff the previous September when he had wanted an election the public had said so clearly it didn't want. With prorogation, Harper had crossed the public's line that he didn't even notice was there. Just as surprising, in response, the Liberals didn't merely attack Harper for his disrespect, but they returned to Ottawa on January 25, the day Parliament had been scheduled to resume. Further, instead of reducing their return to a stunt, they organized round-table forums each day all day for the following three weeks. The forums, open to the media and the public, were on subjects of large public import—the current economy and the economy of the future; poverty, housing, and homelessness; the Afghan detainees; women in Canada today; and on subjects of less predictable public interest—wounded veterans, physically and psychologically, and the obligations of the state; Alzheimer's and dementia; doctors in rural communities. With space and time to fill, the national media did stay in Ottawa, and many of them did come to Parliament Hill. A few attended the sessions, though most did not stay long, and most focused on their BlackBerrys when they were there. They did attend Ignatieff's daily mid-day press conference, where he talked about the issues raised during the morning session. Skipping past that, the media asked him about Afghan detainees, a misstatement by one of the government ministers, or some other news priority that *they* had for the day. By the second week, when the Liberals had proven they were serious, the media became more respectful.

The biggest surprise was the effect the sessions had on the Liberal members themselves. Many Liberal MPs had planned to be in Ottawa only because the Liberal Whip had told them they must be, or only for a day or two because they were organizing one of the forums themselves. But the more sessions they attended, the more they did attend. They had all been involved in expert roundtables before, but usually on subjects about which they, as opposition critics, had some responsibility, and involving experts who were trying to influence and persuade them. These sessions felt different. They were on so many different subjects, and presenting them, session after session, day after day, were fascinating, intelligent people who believed in what they were doing, who believed better was possible, and who believed that maybe these Members of Parliament, this party, and government in general might be able to do something. The Liberal members, more excited than they had been in a long time, left with a resolve that surprised them.

The forums had a similar effect on Ignatieff, who was there almost all day, almost every day. He did not offer the usual leader's greeting, then leave. He gave five or ten minutes of opening comments to help frame the issue of a session, then stayed and listened, constantly making notes. At the end of a session, he responded. It was clear that he had been listening; he highlighted what had struck him most, then suggested the direction the Liberals would take should they become the government. This was Ignatieff at his best—listener, learner, ponderer, sense-maker, meaning-seeker, big-picture-finder. In those three weeks, his confidence growing, he seemed finally to realize: I can be good at this. It might even be fun.

During this time of prorogation, Harper had given Ignatieff his chance. It is hard to imagine how else Ignatieff might have received such a chance, to right himself and discover his way. In the months and years ahead, if Ignatieff does become prime minister, if he becomes a prime minister who governs with a large purpose and leaves behind an important legacy, the turning point will not have been the Montreal Conference or any other moment, it will have been in these three weeks of public forums in January and February 2010 when this country's issues and experts came to Ottawa, and Ignatieff and the Liberals began to find their pride and realize their possibilities.

Prorogation ended, and Governor General Michäelle Jean read the Harper government's Speech from the Throne. The next day, Finance Minister Jim Flaherty delivered his budget. Both were quiet, little-noteworthy affairs. The country had gone through the storm of the recession, another storm was brewing as deficits would need to be fought, but that was not for now. The economy still needed the stimulus of the government's spending, much of which had still not found its way into people's pockets. Ignatieff announced to the media that he would oppose the budget but that he wouldn't bring the government down. To do this, some of his Liberal members wouldn't be present on the day of the vote. But this time for Ignatieff, there was no media ridicule; everyone knew it was the only thing to do. After the parties had said what they always say about a budget, after the votes had been held that left the government still standing, there seemed a pause. After the hit of prorogation, after the feel-good bounce of the Olympics, the Conservatives and Liberals were almost even in the polls.

Behind the scenes, plans were being made. Ignatieff was looking for a slow, steady rise in support for his party and for himself. Next would be the Montreal Conference, then several smaller regional conferences, and in between and after which he would spend lots of time outside Ottawa. Being in so many places so often, he would begin to look like part of the national landscape. He would continue this way through the summer and into the fall, building up toward an election, perhaps in the spring of 2011.

Harper had his own timetable. His most obvious election scenario had to do with the fall of 2010. The G8 and G20 were meeting in Canada over the summer. He would be host, and as host he would sit in the middle of the front row for the pictures. The presidents and prime ministers of the world's great countries would sit around him. They would say the nice things visitors say about their host and their host's country. The Queen would also visit this summer. Michäelle Jean's term was ending, and Harper would appoint a new Governor General. Harper would use the summer to be visible in big ways during an otherwise invisible time. And as summer was ending, and with the first bite of fall, before Ignatieff could emerge from summer in-consequence to find his footing, Harper could drop on him his next attack ads. If Ignatieff wanted more time, why give it to him? If Ignatieff wanted to wait until after the next budget in February 2011, when the stimulus money will all have been spent, when unemployment is still high, when the deficit remains more than $50 billion and cuts will finally have to be made, why let him wait? Besides, in September Harper could say to the public and to his new Governor General that it has been two years since the last election, and two years is about the average life of a minority government. With tough economic and fiscal decisions to make, he needed a mandate from Canadians. The country needed an election.

But Harper has another, less obvious scenario. He has been prime minister for more than four years, yet it doesn't seem that long. With two minority governments, with possible elections and rumoured elections at almost every moment, he seems to have governed almost month to month. He came into office with a distinct right-wing set of beliefs. He believed in small government, privatization, and "traditional" family values. Many Canadians found him "scary," and enough still do that, in spite of the absence of any strong alternative in the Liberals, they have refused to vote him a majority government. Yet he has been able to do whatever he wanted because the Liberals have been too weak to stop him—"support me or bring me down." For Harper, because he has had only minority governments, for those of his supporters who weren't looking for radical changes, it seems he has been able to do all he has done in spite of having only minority governments, and for those who have been looking for radical changes, it seems he hasn't been able to do what they want him to do because of having only minority governments. All this has been to Harper's great good fortune. In fact, a majority government would have been far harder for him. He would have had to deal with different assumptions and much more demanding expectations. His supporters, having suffered through thirteen years of Liberal governments and thirteen years of being abused as right-wing wackos, would insist: *we* won; we have waited long enough; it is *our* turn. If Harper had tried to deliver to those expectations, he would have confirmed the fears of all those Canadians about him. A majority government would have created a clear line of debate, and this debate would have rallied the Liberals to rediscover themselves more purposefully and more quickly. For Harper, it would also have put the focus, and kept the focus, on him.

A prime minister lives under the glare of a ubiquitous spotlight. In such light, anyone's flaws are starkly revealed. With a minority government, with an election around every corner, and with the Liberals unsettled and weak because of this, Harper has been able to shift the spotlight away from himself and onto them. It is the Liberals who have been under the glare most of these Harper years. It is Dion, and now Ignatieff, who have had their flaws so starkly revealed. This glare normally ages a party and a prime minister; it makes the public grow impatient and insist on change. It is now more than four years since Stephen Harper was elected prime minister; about this time the public begins to grow restless and look for a change. Today, Harper seems less worn than Dion did, less worn than Ignatieff does now.

A majority government in 2006 or 2008 would have changed this for Harper. As prime minister, Harper has had all of the advantages and none of the disadvantages of a majority government. Ignatieff has had all of the disadvantages and none of the advantages of a minority government. Harper has been able to do most of what he has wanted to do: to advance support for the military; to cut the GST; to cut the capacity of the federal government; to cut support to social programs for Aboriginals, for health, for women, for child care.

And Harper has been able to do this without looking like a right-wing ideologue. He has avoided turning everything into a right-left fight. The words he uses are virtually identical to those of the Liberals, and often even to those of the New Democrats. He does not bash the bureaucracy; he talks about the dedicated public servants who work diligently for their country, even as he cuts back and limits what they do. He talks about supporting families with his Universal Childcare Benefit, even as its $100 a month benefit per child, with the average cost of child care being $8,000 a year nationally, has had almost no effect on child care. He talks about

Canada's responsibility to the world, using our engagement in Afghanistan as its proud symbol, even as he
pulls out long-term support from Rwanda and Burkina
Faso and other parts of Africa, even as diplomats from
other countries and international non-governmental
organizations ask again and again, "Where is Canada?"
even as he disengages diplomatically on the most
pressing global questions from most of the rest of the
world. He talks about the plight of the unemployed,
even as he resists attempts to extend benefits to most
of those caught in the deeper, harsher unemployment
of the recession. He talks about the good work of social
justice groups, even as he cuts their funding and si-
lences the voices of those who advance their causes.

Harper doesn't spend his time arguing against the
Liberal agenda; instead, he pushes his own. He talks
about the "tax-and-spend," "soft-on-crime" Liberals,
but every party talks about taxing and spending less,
and reducing crime, and so his words sound more like
politics than they do ideology. He has not forced any
fights that seem ideological because he knows most
Canadians don't share his ideology, and he would lose.
He has learned that the only fight to focus on is taxes.

It is not likely that Harper had been aware of this approach in his first few years as prime minister. He certainly didn't seem aware in his earlier years in opposition

and outside government as head of the National Citizens Coalition. But he knows now that if he focuses on taxes, if he can make cutting taxes the issue, everything else falls into place. Then the debate is not about big government or small government, it is about taxes. It is not about important public services that a government provides, or the money it gives to community groups—for literacy or child care—it is about taxes. The debate is not ideological—right or left—it is about taxes. And everybody—right or left—is for cutting taxes. Harper has learned that he can win every ideological fight if he doesn't fight these battles ideologically. If he fights, he loses; if he doesn't fight, he wins.

Harper doesn't need an election in the fall of 2010 to do what he wants to do. He can do that now. He doesn't need a majority. From his point of view, he is better off without one. Without a majority, he can keep his most radical supporters at bay; he can keep the public discourse non-ideological. Harper needs an election in the fall not to do what he wants to do as prime minister. He needs an election in the fall to keep the Liberals in disarray.

The Montreal Conference was called Canada 150: Rising to the Challenge. It was an opportunity not just for Liberals but for Canadians to take stock of their country and the world, to see where we are and where we should be going as we approach our 150th birthday in 2017. It was a chance to bring together interesting, accomplished people to talk to an audience of political media who are rarely exposed, and who rarely expose themselves, to people like them, to a small live gathering of three hundred or so, and to a much larger online gathering connected across the country who would be both spectators to the proceedings by webcast and participants in real time. For the Liberals, it was a chance to show the competence and grasp of Ignatieff, to demonstrate his ease in interacting with big issues and big thinkers, and to show his willingness to hear opinions different from his own, and to do so publicly, even those opinions that might be deeply critical of him or the Liberal Party. It was also Ignatieff's chance to put into the minds of citizens and journalists a question he wanted them to ask themselves: "Can you ever in your life imagine Stephen Harper doing this?"

The conference went mostly as the Liberals had planned. The technology worked. The website facilitator listened to the discussion on the conference floor, monitored the online questions and comments, and when brought in by the moderator interjected with questions and comments appropriate to the discussion, allowing the discussion to flow as if "Mark from

Sackville" or "Dawn from Peterborough" were there. The experts did what they were supposed to do. They talked with seriousness about the present and the future economy, the need for learning to underpin Canada's future prosperity, and the challenge of reconciling a high deficit and costly programs with public needs and expectations. They talked about the aging population, not only as a burden on the health-care system, but as a loss of trained people from an economy that needs more skill, not less.

While most panellists were polite in tone if not in the depth of their criticisms, Robert Fowler was not. A career diplomat and a former Canadian ambassador to the United Nations, Fowler saw Canada's reputation for fairness in foreign policy being sold out "exclusively for domestic purposes," our political parties pandering to one group or another—the Jews, the Tamils—in order to secure their vote. Although Fowler was most critical of the Harper government, he sent his conference audience into a deep cringe with his words, "It seems the Liberals today don't stand for much in the way of principle." He continued, "I have the impression that they will endorse anything and everything that might return them to power, and nothing which won't." As for Afghanistan, "It is time to leave; not a moment, not a life, not a dollar later."

Without anyone having to say so, two words were off the conference's table, banned from the room, incinerated out of existence—*carbon tax*. Stéphane Dion had tried that, and everyone knew the rest of that story. His Green Shift was a *tax*. Any new tax, everyone knew, was political suicide because every other political party could then offer in response a knowingly false or willfully blind story about how stupid and wrong the tax is, and the public will hear what it wants and will accept any false solution to avoid paying another tax. In other words, a carbon tax is not worth discussing. The problem for the panellists was that as they addressed the necessity of connecting energy benefits to actual costs in order to get the pricing and the incentives right, doing nothing, they agreed, would not work, cap and trade would not work, and nothing else would work except a ___ ___, the two words that could not be spoken. Eventually someone did speak those words; then others did too. But each time they did, the words came out with a quivery giggle even before they had been fully expressed, then followed by a full laugh, which was shared by the suddenly liberated conference audience.

The giggle was the sound of outsiders talking to insiders, which said, "I am a scientist or a business person, not a politician, and I know that only a carbon tax can work. But I also see myself, and I want to be seen, as a serious person, and I know that a carbon tax can't work even if it is the only thing that can work because politically it can't work, because I know politics defines what is serious, not science or economics. So when I say the words *carbon tax*, I laugh, to reinforce my reputation to you as a serious person and to make you know that, *wink wink nudge nudge*, I know too. So then we can get back to not talking about the only thing that can work."

Some of the conference's experts on the economy, families, demographics, climate change, and the world were Liberal supporters; many others were not. They were at the conference because they were asked and were given an audience, because they are proud of the reputation they have, a reputation that speaking at this conference would enhance. They were there mostly because what was being discussed was important, and because Canada at 150 years old, and Canada in all the years after, is important. And even if these experts were not optimistic that anything would come of what they said, they were there because they are hopeful because there is no point in being anything else. Although they may have hedged their emotional bets as they spoke about the carbon tax, they were there to say to the Liberals and to any government: "You have to do what needs to be done. If not now, when? If not you, who? If not you, why do you exist?"

Ignatieff had opened the conference; now it was his turn to close it. The conference had highlighted many big questions, he said, that as a party and as a country we must act upon, stressing the word *must*. He focused on three big themes: learning, caring, and the world. He again emphasized the importance of learning, and how learning *must* mean child care, literacy, language training for immigrant families, greater affordability for colleges and universities, and closing the learning attainment gap between Aboriginal and non-Aboriginal children. He talked about the challenge of an aging population. He talked about the need for greater health promotion, and to fight illness and disease at the point where they are most effectively fought—in severity and cost—*before* the fact, with prevention, citing obesity and diabetes as examples. He talked about the need for Canadian global leadership, citing our embarrassment in Copenhagen, where other countries, in trying to put together a last-minute deal, because of the unhelpful role Canada had played earlier in the Conference, purposely did *not* invite Canada into these crucial sessions. "Never again!" Ignatieff thundered. "I want us to be . . . the most international society in the world," he continued. "I'm proud I was out there in the world for the years I was outside. I'm proud of it!" he repeated. His audience roared.

He talked about productivity, and how we *must* focus on "clean tech, renewable energies and energy efficiency" and creating the "right fiscal incentives" to make them work. He talked about a different style of government. His job as prime minister would be to link people together, to link business and government, to link the federal, provincial, and municipal governments, thereby creating networks. That is the way the world of the future will work, he said.

Then Ignatieff paused and changed his pace. He said that no matter what he said at that moment or what anybody else had said this weekend, he knew nobody would be listening unless they believed there was a way to pay for the ideas expressed. Canada's deficit was now at $56 billion a year. His government would meet the challenge of this deficit by freezing corporate income taxes at their current level of 18 per cent, which, Ignatieff said, is 25 per cent lower than the corporate rate in the United States; he would not reduce these rates further to 15 per cent as the Harper government intended, until the deficit was much lower. This approach would generate about $5 billion to $6 billion a year in additional revenues, which would fund these other important priorities. This was his plan. It was respectful of the reality of Canada's large fiscal deficit, and it was respectful of Canada's needs and opportunities in the future.

"I think we changed our politics this weekend," Ignatieff concluded. "I think we changed ourselves."

During a conference, everything seems logical, obvious, and possible. After a conference ends, a political filter descends, and everything seems difficult, unclear, and unlikely. The conference organizers and the conference presenters had done their job; now it was up to the Liberals to do their job. The message of the conference was one of urgency and excitement. It was up to Ignatieff to take this message, and to take his own words, and make them real for Canadians. In his closing press conference, Ignatieff was asked that, because his party might not become government in the next year or two, and the Conservatives might by then have reduced the corporate income tax rate to 16.5 per cent, or to 15 per cent, would Ignatieff's government then raise that tax rate back to 18 per cent? "No," Ignatieff said.

The House resumed in Ottawa the following day. Talk among the Liberals was less about the issues raised at the conference than about what a great conference it had been. During Question Period the week before, Conservative members dismissed Canada 150 as the Liberals' "Spenders Conference." Now they called it "Tax-a-palooza." Everything is about taxes, the Conservatives were again warning. Are you sure you're up for the fight?

For many Canadians, Harper is a political genius. He has made enough huge political mistakes that some have come to question this reputation. But even if he has been dealt a strong political hand, he has still played it masterfully. So long as politics is the only game in town, he is the only game in town.

When politics takes over, nothing else happens. Although a lot seems to go on, not much does. When an athlete gets older and loses his effectiveness, it is said that he "loses his legs." But before he loses his legs, he loses the drive to move his legs. He doesn't see himself so committedly as an athlete anymore. The same is true with a country. The Soviet Union stopped believing in itself and, faced with unblinking pressure, it collapsed. The decadence of Rome is not what undid Rome, it was Romans losing their belief in Rome and, with nothing bigger to focus on, they focused decadently on themselves. This is the same challenge now facing the United States. When politics takes over, it is a symptom of something more disturbing. Politics takes over when there is no other big story around. Loud, fast, pounding, relentlessly going nowhere, *this* politics is "punk politics."

Canada's problem in the past has been that with our immense resources, our proximity to the United States, the skilled, hard-working people who have come as immigrants to our shores, and with the modest understandings we have had of ourselves, we have been able to live a safe, secure, prosperous life with our eyes closed, no matter what the state of our politics. But now, to be what is in us to be, we need more than a different understanding of ourselves; we need a different politics too. And it is this important story of ourselves that will drive a different politics; nothing else will. Politics breeds politics; purpose breeds purpose. If one party believes in something, it pushes other parties to do the same. Our politics will not change unless our understanding of Canada changes. And that understanding will not change only from the actions of our political parties or of our political media. The political media love politics, even this politics, at the same time as they often hate themselves for loving it. This understanding of Canada will emerge out of the back and forth of a national conversation among politicians, the media, and the voices big and small of other Canadians who have lived more, can see more, expect more, and demand more. Harper has laid out the challenge. We can carry on, and, with a little more money in our own pockets, we can do well. And we can continue to do well longer than almost any other country in the world because even with the loss of our manufacturing to China, India, and elsewhere, and even with other unimaginable bumps in the road, any foreseeable world of the future will need our resources, our peace, our stability, and our security.

Someone once said that the world is made up of ironists and passionists. Ironists don't believe important things can be done, so they live on the sidelines at arm's length from the action. Their need is to *be* right. Passionists, on the other hand, do believe important things can be done even if they don't always know how to do them, and so they live at the centre of the action. Their need is to *do* right. The question is, What *right?* Their passion is for what purposes, with what results? In recent years, the political right in Canada and in the United States has offered passion; the political left, until Obama, under the guise of reason, has offered irony. And in a head-to-head fight, even if there are more ironists than passionists, passionists will win. The era of the ironist is over. In Canada, in the United States, in the world, in science, in business, in the arts, in politics, and in matters of conflict, the era of the passionist is beginning.

As Canadians, we can do well, or we can be what we are and do more and better. The future is not just about taxes. It is about what kind of country we want.

BECOMING CANADA

IN A WELL-KNOWN DEMONSTRATION in psychology, subjects are shown a video in which two teams of players, one team wearing white shirts, the other wearing black, move around and pass basketballs to one another. The subjects are asked to count the number of passes made. In the midst of the video, a woman in a gorilla suit walks to the centre of the screen, pounds her chest, then leaves. Focused on counting the number of passes, half of the subjects don't notice the woman in the gorilla suit. The lesson: we see what we are looking for. For decades, focusing on the "Typically Canadian, eh?" version of Canada, we have missed the gorilla.

But that is changing. Many Canadians are now thinking more about their country and their future. They are mostly the young, in universities or fresh into their new careers, and those who are older, in their sixties and more. They are an odd alliance, these twenty-somethings and sixty-somethings, yet they need each other. The sixty-somethings give the twenty-somethings confidence that they are right to feel as they do, about their life and about their planet, and have the right to do something about it. The twenty-somethings give the sixty-somethings new purpose, new energy, and new belief that important changes might happen this time. They make them feel young again. There is another voice too, of many different ages, most prominently in the arts, where writers, playwrights, directors, musicians, some of whom were not born in Canada, are giving expression to their own unique Canadian learnings and experiences, telling stories and doing so in ways the world is clamouring for. These artists are telling of the Canada within them, paying no attention to history as it was related to them or to critics who tell them not to bother. It is the same in business, though to a much lesser extent, and in science, though for different reasons. In today's global world, talent and ambition, like air and water, ignore borders and go where they want to go.

This older generation had grown up expecting more and had been disappointed. Now, having seen the world and seeing Canada as we are today, this generation sees where the future is going, and it *knows*. This younger generation knows that the future belongs to them—it is *their* Canada, *their* world—and says, *Why not?* Both are earnest; one is at a pre-ironic age, the other post-ironic. To that paralyzing understanding of the past—"We are just Canada"—their response is calm and defiant: "We are more than this."

The older were born mostly in the decade after the Second World War into a Canada of possibilities. Many grew up in suburbs in new houses surrounded by many other new houses, with new schools and churches and parks not far away. Many grew up with middle-class parents who hadn't gone to university and had never dreamed they would, whose biggest hope was that their children would graduate from university and create the unimaginably wonderful Canada and world that only university graduates could create. This generation grew up lucky and knew they were lucky, surrounded by a world of destruction and deprivation—the relentless poverty of Asia, the humanity-choked hopelessness of China and India, the impossibility of Africa, the corrupt sadness of Central and South America, and a Europe so fundamentally flawed it had twice tried to annihilate itself in thirty years.

These sixty-somethings grew up in a Canada that was a neighbour to the greatest power on Earth, the United States of America, to the greatest *place* on Earth—New York, Hollywood, cars, stars, where everything was bigger and more exciting. The United States was a good place, a decent place of freedom and prosperity, where everyone had a chance and where even the poor would do well someday.

These sixty-somethings grew up in a Canada where classrooms had on their walls a map of the world on which the pink outline of Canada was so big, so much bigger than the pink of Britain and the purple of France, almost as big as the purple of the Soviet Union, and bigger than the yellow of the United States and China. To these Canadians, Canada was big, and they knew that if a country had space, population would come. Importance would come. If a country had space, it had resources. Even if a lot of that space was cold and remote, someday it wouldn't be. Frontiers were made to be tamed and turned into something special. Space was destiny. It was only a matter of time, and Canada's time would come. These people had no doubt. To them, the United States emerging out of the Second World War was a country of greatness realized on the way to something greater. Canada was a country of greatness imagined, and greatness imaginable.

But by the 1960s, things began to feel different to them. Neither the United States nor Canada was living up to its special promise. For the United States, it was the problems of race, the Vietnam War, the Cold War, the materialism of a consumer society, the conformism of the suburbs, the corporate and governmental abuses of power that had brought about the rise of Ralph Nader and Watergate. For Canada, the disappointment had to do mostly with being so irresistibly tied to the United States, with the southward drain of Canada's stars, not only in business, science, sports, and the arts but in every field. Government and corporate decisions, it seemed, always were made in Washington, New York, or Dubuque. With all our special promise, these Canadians wondered, Is this what Canada is about?

When their country stumbled, the United States mythmakers turned angry. Ours—our writers and media stars—turned cynical and ironic. No matter what we do, it seemed to them—anything, everything—we can't pull it off. *Typically Canadian, eh?* When CBC Radio icon Peter Gzowski ran a contest on his program for a phrase that best described our national identity, the winning phrase was: "As Canadian as possible—under the circumstances." Funny, wise-sounding—years later we are still under the thumb of these old myths and mythmakers and their official understanding of Canada, even if the world and Canada have changed dramatically, even if Canadians are ready to see themselves differently. But this suffocating thumb of the past is losing its power.

As for these twenty-something Canadians, their experiences and life circumstances are different. They are from almost every country on Earth. Their reference point beyond Canada is not the United States; it is the world. They connect to the world everyday in their classrooms and offices, in their neighbourhoods, in their clothes, their food, and their music. They travel to everywhere and anywhere online. They digitally inhabit any setting they want. They are old enough to know enough of the present to imagine the future, and yet they are young enough not to be overburdened by the past. They are young enough not yet to have overwhelmed what they feel with explanation; they are young enough to be outraged by the outrageous and excited by the exciting. And they know that the tough and necessary global fights of the future—climate change, human rights, poverty, starvation—demand outrage and excitement. Although most of these young people may not be interested in politics, almost all of them are interested in the world.

Older adults say these young people have turned every excess into entitlement and need, and are only interested in what job they will have when they graduate, and how much money they will make. But go to a university campus and give these young people a reason to talk about their country and their world. They want most of all to talk about the environment, especially climate change, and about human rights. To them, both climate change and human rights are fundamental matters of fairness, and to them, they are one and the same. With climate change, it is fairness to all living beings, fairness from their parents to them, fairness from them to their own children and grandchildren; fairness to the future. Every person has been given the privilege of life, and no one has the right to take that privilege away from anyone else, present or future. With regard to human rights, this generation has grown up learning to treat adults as equals. It does not matter to these young people that an adult is older, nor that the adult is bigger, stronger, was born into the right family, has a university degree, and makes lots of money. "I am a human being and you are a human being," these young people say. "That is what matters; that is all that matters. If you earn my respect, I will give you my respect. If you expect it, but do not earn it, I will withhold my respect." To these young people, why should it be any other way?

Why, then, should it matter that someone was born in Sudan or Afghanistan, Myanmar or Canada? We all have rights befitting of being human. We all have a right to live undiminished by hunger, disease, or prejudice. We all have a right to exploit every talent and capacity within us. And no one has the right to stop us, not for economic reasons, not for political or military reasons, not for any reason at all. So when these young people think and talk about Canada and the world, they do so with great propriety. "This is *my* life, *my* country, *my* world," they say. "I have every right to make it all it can be, and you have no right to make it anything less." We are good, these young people are saying, and the right story of ourselves as a person, a country, and a world will make us better. And we have no right not to make it better.

The old story of Canada, and the story of the United States, didn't change much after the mid-1960s, year after year—until Obama. During the 2008 campaign, Obama spoke to the pride, the guilt, and the hope of Americans, and he challenged them: "We are better than this." And the American people wanted to believe him, and believe in him, because they wanted to believe in "America" again. Canadians watched Obama almost as closely as Americans. Indeed, had they the chance, a higher percentage of Canadians likely would have voted for Obama than did Americans. Obama spoke to that same profound, unsettled feeling and that same aspiration and hope inside Canadians.

Look at us, these Canadians younger and older say. We are now 34 million people, one of the world's largest economies and one of the world's richest nations. We have a huge and abundant landmass amid a world of congested countries. We are safe, secure, and stable. We are clean, civil, modest, polite, and respectful—all those qualities others ascribe to us that sometimes make us squirm. We are dull and boring, still others say. But compared to whom? The United States? "Boring" meaning no big surprises; no rampant disease, no terrorist attacks, no hurricanes, no earthquakes, no major economic or political disasters of our own making? A country without tabloid extremes? In Canada, we can plan for tomorrow, and count on tomorrow, when billions around the world cannot. We can put to one side most of the big distractions that can bring family and career to a halt, and we can live life fully. All those qualities about us that embarrass us a little—all those qualities the world is dying for. And because of our Aboriginal history, because of countless Aboriginal nations and their challenge to survive, because of our French and English past of different languages, cultures, religions, and laws, because today we have people inside our borders from almost everywhere—we are a country that has learned to live with and accept difference, and to learn from difference, when in the rest of the world difference often means guns and blood.

Once, the world was a disconnected place, disconnected by distance, by geography—oceans, mountains, deserts—by culture and customs, language and laws, even by thought—each of them, all of them, reinforcing and exaggerating difference. Now the world is connected, and a connected world, a global world, cannot be about difference. A connected world can be only about getting along, about living together, and about the instincts and the instruments for doing that. This is Canada. Countries come and go, prominent for a time, then pushed to the sidelines in another. History is a long time. Whatever Canada has been in the past, we will be far more in the future. The world knows it, and now we need to know it too.

Would the world be as good a place if Canada didn't exist? What matters about Canada now, and what will matter to the world in the future? Is it Canada as a northern country, with the great impact—economic, environmental, cultural, and military—that the north will have on the world's future, and the chance for us to do things better this time? Perhaps.

Is it Canada as an environmental model? Our forests, lakes and rivers, mountains and prairies are what others think of first when they think of us. The environment as beauty, the environment as riches, the environment as both beauty and riches together in a sustainable way? Perhaps.

Is it Canada as innovator? The world is not about knowing—it is about learning. The sun revolves around the Earth until we learn that it doesn't. What we know now is just a placeholder for what we will learn someday in the future. Is it that our population is more broadly educated per capita than almost anywhere else in the world, and our immigrants from everywhere bring their centuries of learning with them—together generating great innovation? Possibly.

What is that bigger story of ourselves? What makes us special? Because the United States, Britain, France, and others have found *their* common story in their history, it seems that we must too. Because no such vivid story has emerged from our history, it seems that we have skipped a step and need to go back before we can go ahead. And we have tried that, with the CBC series *Canada: A People's History*, with *Heritage Minutes*, and with recent histories like John Ralston Saul's *A Fair Country*. Yet none of these histories has even begun to shake our old understanding of ourselves. Too many people and too many groups have too much of a stake in that past. French-English, East-West: when we focus on old fights, they become new fights. Finding a new common story is not about defeating old stories, it is about writing new ones that make the old ones seem less important. We have learned the long way and the hard way. Our past can deepen and enrich our sense of ourselves. But we need to find a common story, we need to search for our future, in what we are now. History is not only about writing the past. History is also about writing the future.

And what we are now is very good. It is not easy to be respectful; it is not easy accepting people different from ourselves. But perhaps our biggest achievement is that we have resisted the almost impossible pull to be like the United States. The United States is a spectacularly successful country. We share the same landmass. What except a perverse, knee-jerk, anti-Americanism would keep us from wanting to imitate their every move? Our history, however, is a little different. Our land and our climate are harsher. Our success has not been so certain. We learned in the past that we needed our neighbour and our neighbour needed us. This reality has made us a little more forgiving, generous, and humble. The individual and individual rights matter to us, but collective rights do too. Some things have to be done together; sometimes government needs to play a role. We have accepted higher taxes to deliver to remote and disadvantaged places what we believe every Canadian should have. We were never going to be the richest, and so our pursuit of wealth has been tempered by other aspects of life that also make life feel good. The gap between our rich and our poor, though much wider than in Western Europe and though too uncomfortably wide for our own sense of ourselves, is still far less than in the United States.

We have also said no to Vietnam, no to Iraq, and yes to medicare. We take great pride in having a public health-care system. In poll after poll, almost embarrassingly, we describe it as central to our identity. A few years ago, the "father of medicare," Tommy Douglas, was named as CBC's "greatest Canadian." Yet surely there is more to us than a public health-care system. This pride we express is not only in the system itself; it is in the fact that we created it, it matters, and it is right. And the people of the United States, at least until Obama's bloody and watered-down health-care victory in 2010, couldn't do it themselves. It would have been so much easier for us not to have tried to create and build this system during all the years the United States was in the health-care wilderness, yet it wasn't possible for us not to try. Our public health-care system is too emblematic of us. Whether as Canadians we are generous or modest or humble, we are at least realistic and pragmatic. We know that when blizzard or flood or crop failure come, and they will come, there are limits to what we can do; it doesn't matter how rich or powerful we are. It is the same with illness and disease. Americans believe that every American has an answer for everything, or should have; Americans believe that they can do everything themselves, or should be able to. As Canadians, if we give up on our public health-care system, we would be giving up on a fundamental understanding of ourselves as Canada—that we need each other; that we are good for each other—something that *is* central to our identity. This we have refused to do. But being "not them," being "not America," is not enough.

There is also something special in the way we get along in Canada. In a global world, we can no longer avoid each other. All those different cultures and languages, traditions and customs, all those different experiences and backgrounds, all those deep-in-the-bone stereotypes and prejudices, conflicts and misunderstandings, all the water of centuries and centuries gone under the bridge—suddenly, now, they are all in one place, here and everywhere. The biggest challenge of a global world is not economic, military, or environmental. The biggest challenge is living together. And in Canada we are living together with difference better than in any other country in the world. Why? And why does that matter so much?

Canada was not created out of revolution. We have no history of civil war. On matters that might have led to the breakup of our country, we held two referendums. For nearly twenty years we have had in our federal Parliament a major party whose purpose is an independent Quebec. Our instinct is not to fight; it is to work things out. Immigrants new to the country who carry with them histories of bloody hostility—often against those who are now their next-door neighbours—are given a quiet, subtle, but insistent message when they arrive: *We get along here.*

This message wouldn't have mattered much in an age of empire. Then the world was about power and might. The strong did not have to get along; the weak did. The strong could believe they were right and act as if they were right because they could impose their right. In Canada, early settlers lived in huge spaces, in small groups in which no one group was large enough even to pretend to dominate another—the "losers of history," some have called them—French Canadians, Loyalists, displaced Highland Scots, Irish fleeing the potato famine. We needed one another to survive. We had to get along, and so we did. The age of empire made Canada seem weak and irrelevant. But in today's post-empire age, power and might are not enough. The strong cannot impose right so easily; the weak are numerous and not so weak that they can be imposed upon. Everyone has to find accommodation; we all have to get along. Canadians know how; many others do not. The age of globalism makes Canada remarkable and crucial.

In an age of empire, homogeneity was good. In the age of globalism, it is not. We can see the importance of diversity all around us in our natural world. About a century ago, town squares and university campuses were planted with tall and majestic elms. Then disease wiped out most of them. The few that survived made it, in part, because other species of trees were planted in their midst. The genetic diversity of nature brought adaptability and resilience. Diversity, it turned out, was good, healthy, and necessary. The monoculture of elms could not survive. The multiculture of elms, oaks, maples, and others survive and thrive.

The American idea of the "melting pot" had seemed so compelling to many Canadians. People from everywhere, coming together, having a place, making an American life for themselves, their languages, cultures and traditions gradually "melting" out of existence. Again, it would have been so easy for Canadians to think the same way. But those settlers who came to Canada were not so numerous, and our established culture was not so defined when others arrived, and so we imposed less. In the 1930s, author John Murray

Gibbon described Canada as a "mosaic" of cultural pieces, each piece separate and distinct, each engaging the others in mutual respect, each retaining its own identity yet each contributing to the country as a whole—with English and French at the centre of that whole. This image, proudly different from a "melting pot," stuck, and in 1971 Canada became the first country in the world to declare multiculturalism as official state policy. This policy, without doubt, has helped to preserve the identity and strength of many ethnic communities across the country. Today, walk around the Vancouver suburb of Surrey or the Toronto suburbs of Brampton or Agincourt and, block after block, you might think you had been dropped into India or China. But today we don't live a multicultural life in Canada. We have moved beyond that to something else, to something new in the world. Newcomers to Canada are not only changed by Canada, they are changing Canada. They are making Canada into something it has never been. The dynamic of Canada is not one of groups existing and functioning separate and distinct from one another. It is not one group disappearing into another with little effect. The Canadian dynamic is far more interesting, far more challenging, and far more important. It is a blend, a mix, neither English, nor French, nor Italian, Chinese, or Indian, but something new. In an increasingly global world, Canada has become the world's first global culture. Canada has become a "multiculture."

For older Canadians, and for younger Canadians too, this new importance for Canada comes as a great surprise. As a country, we did not arrive where we are through any plan. We lived our life circumstances, adapted with each turn in the road, and this is what we have become. Now we find ourselves in this strange position where the line on the world-graph and the line on the Canada-graph have come together. We are going where the world is going. We are what the world needs. All those qualities that embarrass us a little—being civil, modest, polite and respectful, getting along, having a history without the glory of revolution or empire or civil war—all qualities the world is dying for, that a global world needs, that the future needs.

Noted historian Margaret MacMillan has said that the writing of history began in the 1800s. In an age of power and glory and empire, history was the story nations and governments wanted to have written. Today, attempting to live up to the glories of that old story will only kill us all. For tomorrow's world, nations and governments need to have written a new story, a new history that reflects this global world and where we are going, that accommodates many cultures and many languages, that accepts and can live with differences, that highlights getting along. A new story, an aspirational story, that helps us get to where we are irresistibly going, and successfully. For Canada, the absence in the past of a strong, central story, a strong, central narrative, has allowed us to be what we are, to become what we have become. What had always seemed our problem has become our great good fortune. Canada is where the world is going.

We are a crucial, living experiment. If a global world can't work in Canada, it won't work anywhere. Canada matters, and Canada will matter more in the future. As Canadians, we need to know this about ourselves, not to become complacent, but to become the opposite, to become ambitious, to take on the large questions of the future—climate change, human rights, poverty, starvation—the way this "Canada" would, the Canada that is the most global country in a global world, the Canada of 2010 and of the future.

"CANADA"

WHAT CAN THIS CANADA BE? It is not presumptu-
ous to talk about Canada and "the world" together. The
world is no longer a grandiose "other." The world is a
natural, normal, routine part of the daily existence of
Canada and of every other country. To think about
Canada, we need to think about the world. And the
world's future, it is clear, will depend on learning and
on getting along. How can Canada help to make this
future for ourselves and for the world?

Once, we were a country defined by winter, geography, and distance. Then we were a country defined also
by our French and English relationship, by difference
and relative equality, and by the instinct for accommodation that had to follow. Now and in the future,
we will also be defined by the many diverse peoples
within our borders, by the learning they have brought,
by the challenge they represent, by the possibilities

they provide, by the changes they are making, and by what we create together.

Visitors who come to Canada aren't prepared for the sights they see. They expect Niagara Falls, they expect the Rockies, they expect lakes and trees, they expect modern cities. They don't expect all the different colours of skin, nor all the hijabs, saris, and dashikis visible on the same street at the same time. They are amazed and worried by the sights they see. They think of their own home countries. If they are African, they might think of the hundreds of thousands of refugees who have crossed into their countries because of conflicts near their borders, and the temporary camps they have created that now, ten or fifteen years later, are permanent and hopeless. If they are Asian, they might think of the internal strife between their own citizens, driven by culture or religion or history, that seems never-ending, with worse imaginably yet to come. If they are European, they might think of their own experiences with non-European immigrants; they see the riots and the protests, they see the "us" and the "them," and they don't see how this mix can end well. The multiculture of Canada couldn't work in their home countries. How can it work here? But a multiculture must work here because a global world must work, because we are already too far down a global path with too little to hold us back and too much propelling us forward. A multiculture must work here in Canada because we are also too far down our own path, and we have no choice. Even if we wanted to return to an English-French existence, it is too late. To try to go back would create greater division and conflict. Again, as we have done throughout our history, we need to live our life circumstances and make this work. To do so, we have to make the immigrant experience work, not only for the immigrant but for this Canada and for all of us.

Once, we understood immigration differently. Once, we saw immigrants as cheap labour for rich employers to make things and to do things cheaply, to allow all of us, immigrants included, to buy things and to do things cheaply. Immigration was also the fulfillment of our human obligation to give everybody a chance. Everybody came from somewhere else, even the Aboriginal peoples of every nation. Everybody's ancestors at some time left somewhere and arrived somewhere else with little. For the receiving country, letting these immigrants inside their door meant that their side of the bargain had been met. For the immigrant, their obligation was to do the rest: to accept whatever faced them, to suffer whatever hardship, to work hard, to expect nothing from others, and to make a life for themselves. In time, in Canada, they would learn English or French;

in time, they would learn new customs and improve their lot. They had to be patient, and they had to be willing to be patient. They would have children, and their children would go to school. Their children would learn English or French, and learn it without an accent. They would make friends with other kids who spoke English or French. They would begin to live new customs and ways; they would wear new clothes; they would begin to fit in. Better educated, they would grow up and do different jobs; they would live in different neighbourhoods; they would have more and better chances. They would have different dreams.

For the immigrant family, it was the job of the first generation to take the chance, to make the break, to come to Canada, then to make a beginning, to put down roots, to nurture wings, to begin the future. It would take more than one generation. For the most part, immigrants expected the bargain and accepted it. They came with little formal education; no country offered much formal education at the time. They did the kind of "unskilled" jobs—labouring for the men, house-cleaning or factory work for the women—that they had done in their own native lands. Language was no barrier to their work; they had the strong back they needed. There were exceptions, mostly tradespersons from Britain or Central Europe who were recruited for jobs too few Canadians could do. But for the great majority, with hope but little expectation and doing the jobs they were trained for, when life in Canada changed only slowly, there was some disappointment, though little anger or despair.

The situation is different now. In most countries, formal education is widely offered into high school years and beyond. Canada's immigration standards, for the most part, now require advanced levels of schooling. Many immigrants are well educated and well trained. In their home countries, they held high-skilled jobs and earned the status and pride of high-achievers. They were special, and they are used to being special. Once in Canada, language became a barrier for them in trying to do the work they had done before. Medical doctors and professional engineers in their native countries, they would need to return to school to do the same in Canada, but, now with spouses and children, they can't. So they work in kitchens and drive cabs. It's a living, but they didn't grow up expecting only to prepare the ground for a next generation. *They* were the next generation. In their old home country, they had been on their way. And more than they are Russians, Indians, or even Canadians, they are "professionals." This is how they see themselves. This is where their pride and satisfaction resides, where they fit in and belong. With hope and also high expectations, and not doing the jobs they were trained for, many are disappointed, angry, and often in despair.

Yet in the mind of most Canadians, the old immigrant bargain remains: we have allowed you into the country and the rest is up to you. Work hard and every generation after you will reap the rewards. But there is a better and necessary bargain to be made. Many of these new immigrants are not only highly educated, they have the habits and attitudes of success. They need only the language, and a little training, and someone to invest in them for a brief time until they begin to acquire these skills too. They need rigorous preparation and training programs provided by government and rooted in language development. Their kids need enhanced English as a Second Language programs in school. The preparation of these immigrants, in fact, can begin even earlier. In their own home countries, their visa applications to Canada often take many months, even years, to be approved. This otherwise frustrating time can be used by embassies and consular offices to help applicants ready themselves for their new life in Canada. Some of this transition work is already being done; all of it can be expensive. If we understand an immigrant in the old way, why incur the cost? But if we see the immigrant now as a source of important new national learning, as an instrument to connect deeper and more broadly into the world and into the world economy, creating over time the kind of relationships that generate intended or accidental but important outcomes, and if we see in the immigrant's success or failure the success or failure of this Canadian experiment, our answer will be very different.

This Canada needs to approach immigration with more focus and rigour. After immigrants arrive in Canada, beyond the transition courses and English as a Second Language programs for the children, this Canada must help these immigrants fit in. Once, neighbourhoods functioned far more like self-contained communities. But in recent times, many community institutions have grown weaker, or are gone altogether. Traditional churches have fewer members; it is the same with service clubs and parent-school groups. City recreation programs have been cut back. How do newcomers come to belong? In many cases, it is through immigrants' groups—Somalis, Filipinos, Koreans—coming together, organizing their own institutions, especially their own churches. Through their churches they set up other programs and services for seniors and for their own children, and language and pre-employment classes for working-age adults. Many immigrant groups have created vital new communities for themselves, the kind that long-standing Canadian communities themselves in recent years have been seeking to re-create, with little success.

Most Canadians live in areas of one hundred thousand people or more. Most schools in these areas have kids from many different countries; many more will in the future. Schools must come to understand the remarkable, total learning environment they provide. Schools are not only teachers, books, and subject courses; schools are students, and students are receptacles of immense, diverse learning. If we see a school only as a place where a province-approved curriculum is delivered, often with great difficulty, to students who speak imperfect, accented English and who have been educated under widely varying curricula, we see only problems and challenges. If we see a school also as a place of widely diverse experiences and learning, we see excitement and possibilities.

Today, if you go inside almost any high school in most of these urban areas, if you go into the school's lunchroom, you find a disturbing sight. You see kids from many different countries—Sri Lanka, India, Vietnam, Guatemala, Somalia, Philippines, Jamaica, Haiti— sitting at tables, eating entirely separate and apart from each other. In a classroom, kids of different backgrounds have to sit next to one another. They might never speak to each other; they rarely become each other's best friends. But over time, at least, these kids are getting used to difference. Often unconsciously, they come to learn to deal with difference. Difference comes to matter less and less until it is hardly noticed at all. These kids are learning about the world, and they are experiencing the world, before they ever leave the boundaries of their own classroom. Day after day, they are in rehearsal for living in the global world of the future. This is Canada.

And why are these kids not at each other's throats the way their ancestors have been for generations in their own home countries—Serbs and Croats, Tamils and Sinhalese? When there is one overwhelming majority group, that group knows its power and often imposes it. When there is one overwhelming minority group, that group knows its absence of power and knows its vulnerability. But when there are many groups, when even the largest group is not so much larger than the others, when its power to win any fight is not so clear, it doesn't take the chance. When even the smallest group is not so much smaller than the others, when its weakness is not so clear, it is not so at risk. In a school and outside a school, when there are people from so many places, power and the absence of power cease to be what defines a relationship. This is Canada.

All this is imperfect in reality. There are sometimes gangs, though rarely inside the schools. There are "incidents"—acts of violence or threats of violence—which make us worry and wonder about this Canada. We have seen the riots and burning buildings in the suburbs of Paris. Why not us? Outside of schools, if an ethnic group is large enough, it will self-segregate in one area of a city and take it over—shops, restaurants, businesses, their non-English, non-French signs everywhere. Once there had been Chinatown, Greektown, and Little Italy, now there is also Little India, Little Jamaica, Koreatown, and many others. But after the first generation of immigrants, while most of the shops and businesses remain, many of the nearby residents disperse to other parts of a city and the schools become more mixed. Although this multiculture existence can seem always to be on the edge of breaking down, it doesn't break down. We are not France; we are not Britain. New immigrant groups in France or Britain are large enough to feel strong, yet, overwhelmed by the much larger, more established society, they feel frustrated and angry. They feel trapped. No longer what they were, they feel themselves unable to be what they came to France or Britain to be. Canada's new immigrant groups are large enough to feel strong, but feeling less overwhelmed by a smaller, less established society, feeling less trapped, they are less frustrated and angry. The difference can seem subtle; it is profound.

We mustn't assume that the problems we see in France or Britain will be our problem one day. We mustn't look to France or Britain or the United States for our answers. They see difference, assume difference, legislate for difference, reinforce difference, and in doing so generate the frustration and anger of difference and create more difference. In Canada, if we act as they do and not as what we are, we will become what they are. And we will fail, with far greater consequences.

In Canada, we are more vulnerable. In a less populated country with a less established society and culture, when small groups of immigrants live separate and apart, they pose little problem to the healthy dynamic of the country. When those groups become larger, in some cases growing by tens of thousands a year, and remain separate and apart, that is a problem. With books and newspapers in Punjabi, Chinese, or Russian, even television stations, food stores, businesses, churches, theatres, and community halls, it is now much easier to live almost entirely within the language and culture of your own native country, as if you had never left. As an ethnic group, it is your decision, made easier or harder by how the larger society around you treats you. And if your new life in Canada doesn't have a place for you, why not live your old life where you are? You can live separate and apart, you can fester grievances, you have in your hands the power to destroy. And you have in your hands the power and the opportunity to create something new. Multiculturalism was the right story for another time, but it is not the right story now. Multiculturalism makes the weak strong enough to survive, but multiculturalism makes the relatively strong formidable enough to weaken and divide the whole. New immigrant groups need not give up their old stories, but they need to find new ones too, in Canada, stories that include and excite them, in which they can see themselves and see that they matter. It is the same for any group that feels itself separate from the mainstream, for Quebeckers, for Albertans. If there is no big, compelling story of Canada, why not only a Quebec story, why not only an Alberta story, why not only an Indian or a Chinese story? That big compelling story is the multiculture of Canada.

When teachers and students come to discover the specialness of this Canada, they will begin to imagine its possibilities in their own schools. In history, English, or drama class, teachers will get students to tell their life stories. Not only the stories of their lives in other places but their lives in Canada too. Not only stories of difference but stories that uncover commonality and connection. Students will organize after-school clubs and create other activities and expressions of themselves we cannot yet imagine. Slowly, perhaps not even knowingly, students will feel a greater pride; they will feel that they matter as who they were, and as who they are becoming. Along with other kids born in other countries and those born in Canada, they will feel proud of what they are creating together. Schools make class trips to other parts of the country and student exchanges allow for one student to live for a time with another student's family in another province or another country. These exchanges, however, are severely limited by available time and expense. But what about student exchanges not so limited by time or expense, for a week perhaps, between students who may live only a block apart, between a Sri Lankan student and one from Russia or China or Canada? Imagine what those students would learn and what their families would learn? Imagine what that would mean for their futures? Imagine what that would mean for Canada? And when governments come to understand the specialness of this Canada, imagine how they will deal differently with these immigrant groups. To highlight their importance, instead of focusing on how they are different one from another, pandering to them to gain their support, they will highlight their importance in creating this unique multiculture of Canada. When we think of ourselves a certain way—as schools, churches, businesses, community groups, and governments— we begin to act that way, and we become what we are.

So much has happened already. In metropolitan Canada fifteen years ago, even ten years ago, if you walked down a street and someone walked past you wearing a hijab or a dashiki you did a double-take. Now walk down that same street, pass somebody wearing those same clothes, wearing anything, and there is no double-take. There are almost no double-takes anymore. We have already experienced so many variations of all the different colours and different attires so many times before. Black and white, and all the colours in between, have become an unjarring blend of colour that seems natural and normal to us. Difference still matters, but difference now is rarely the most important thing.

If you travel outside Canada where English or French is not the first language spoken, if you talk to someone in their native language that is not your own, even if you say a well-practised phrase in that language with (objectively) little accent, most people will struggle to understand you. If someone from outside Canada travels here and does the same thing, most Canadians will understand easily. We are used to accents; we are used to difference; they are not. This is Canada.

Getting along, inside our borders and outside, is central to our future. So is learning. As parents, we know that unimaginable change is coming, and when we look at our kids, who, to our own eyes, seem so challenged by today, we worry. We want more than anything to know that in the future they will be all right. But we can't know that. We can give them some money to help them ease their way into that future. But money gets spent. The only security and the only opportunity we can offer them is learning. When their world changes in the future, if our kids have in them the capacity, the patience, and the desire to learn, if they have in them the willingness to give up what they know for what they don't know, they will be fine. They will be as fine as anyone can make them.

We are learning beings. From our first breath to our last breath, we learn. We do things, and in doing those things we see, we hear, we feel, and we connect all that to other things we have already learned, and we learn some more. Then we adapt, and we do those things better. For companies, in a workplace, it is the same—we provide a service, we make a product, and so we see, we hear, we feel, and we connect that to other things we have learned, and we learn some more. Then we adapt, and we do those things better. Then we learn some more. And the more we know, the more we are able to learn.

We need to think about everything we do as learning. We need to approach everything we do as learning. We provide a system of parental leave to enable parents to spend more time with their newborn child, to know that child better so they can become better teachers for their child, so their child will become a better learner. Through our health-care system, we offer all mothers a better chance to deliver healthy, full-term babies, so their babies can begin life at the same starting line as other babies, so those babies can learn as well, and so those babies don't experience life always with the backs of others in front of them. We offer programs for low- and middle-income families to provide them the food, shelter, and other basics that are essential to their children's and to their own learning. We have early learning and child care to provide our children with an additional safe, stimulating place to experience other kids and other adults. We organize clubs, sports, and after-school programs to give kids more and different opportunities to learn. We balance budgets and keep down inflation to encourage investment, to encourage new and better opportunities for learning. We create tax provisions to encourage companies to write off old equipment to buy the newest, most-advanced equipment, to further the skills development, to further the learning, of our workers. We provide broadband access into rural and remote areas to allow for distance education for students and distance learning for everyone. Through grants, subsidies, and donations, we encourage research, innovation, science, and technology to support new learning. We are what we learn; we will be what we learn tomorrow.

We need to see ourselves as a learning society. Any developed country can focus on school systems, child care, research, scholarships, healthy babies, capital cost allowances, and parental leave. But today, perhaps more than anything else, learning is about having a seat at the "learning table." It is about making sure as a person, as a company, and as a country that we are around and involved when the best learning happens. In Canada, we can often provide that learning table ourselves, with money, equipment, and technology to attract top researchers and top learners from other countries. Many countries can do the same, but few can offer a safe, secure, and stable place to live and to work where learning can happen undistracted, and fewer still can offer a place to live and to work inside the unique multiculture and learning environment that is Canada.

There are other ways for us to earn our way to that table too. Other countries trust us. Militarily or economically, we have no history with them of using or abusing our power. We have no history with them as a colonizer. With them, our history is one of listening, discussing, negotiating, compromising, not insisting that everything be our own way, but working with them toward some resolution. That makes us welcome at almost any table, almost everywhere in the world, on matters of the economy and security, but also on more and more issues that have to be worked on globally or they cannot be worked on at all. In matters of infectious diseases, with global pandemics like H1N1, it is often too late to respond after an outbreak begins. Conditions need to be monitored closely where outbreaks might originate. Scientists need to talk to one another, and trust the competence and motivations of one another. They have to work together. In Canada, at labs like VIDO-InterVac at the University of Saskatchewan, scientists study and test new or re-emerging diseases, then they develop and test vaccines, working with others. As Canadians, it is our instinct and our attitude to work together. It is our global reputation, not only in science, but in business, in the arts, in matters of diplomacy, and that is not the reputation of many other countries. Others are comfortable with us, and we are comfortable with them. Like most other countries, we don't have all the resources to do everything; we have to co-operate. More and more the biggest breakthroughs don't happen with one person working heroically and single-mindedly. These breakthroughs require teams of people, of different backgrounds, different specialities, different perspectives and approaches, playing different roles, often in different places, working like a team. We are good at this. These Canadian qualities put us at the table and allow us to learn. As celebrated pianist and conductor Daniel Barenboim said, "Listening to the other" is what makes an orchestra function. It is the same for a team. It is the same for a global world.

Today's problems and today's opportunities are too big to handle alone. Collaboration, co-operation, working together—this is where the world is going. With more well-trained Canadians from more different parts of the world, with a deeper, prouder understanding of ourselves as the most global country in a global world, we will be even better co-workers and co-learners in the future. This is Canada.

Ahead, this Canada will have another significant role to play. Even in a global world, the United States remains the world's most important country. It will continue to have more impact on the world than any other country in matters of economy, security, the environment and climate change, and in determining the spirit, style, and direction of international relationships. The United States can be a constructive or destructive force. How well the world will function as a global world will depend in large measure on the United States. How well the United States does will depend, in part, on Canada.

To the great majority of the world's countries, Canada seems joined to the American hip. At an international gathering, when a point is made about the United States, and then about other countries and no reference is made to Canada, when that oversight is raised, the response invariably is, "Oh yeah, and Canada." It is assumed that our experience is the United States' experience. It comes as a great surprise to these other countries to discover that our experience with the United States is much like their own. Between countries, a relationship is not so much defined by common language, by similar culture, or by shared landmass as it is by power. When the United States negotiates with Argentina or Kenya or Canada over some matter, the interaction may seem like a negotiation, even like a talk between friends, but if negotiations don't go its way, the United States pulls out its "power card" and does what it wants to do. And it rarely gets what it wants because of the ill will this generates. Between countries, so long as one country has the power, it is almost impossible for that country not to use it.

The United States still thinks it has power it doesn't have. This is not the Cold War, where on one side are scores of countries aligned under the United States banner pitted against scores of countries aligned on the other side. Without the "other side," there is no "side." Without a compelling external threat, except for periodic ad hoc "coalitions," everyone mostly goes his or her own way. And on one's own, the powerful become much less powerful.

There is nobody better than Canada at explaining the United States to the rest of the world, and nobody better than Canada at explaining the rest of the world to the United States. This Canada, with greater global self-awareness and greater understanding of its own importance, can play an even more significant role. The United States likes to talk about working together with the world; it likes to talk about "allies" and "friends." It understands itself and wants to be under-stood as part of the great brotherhood of the world's people. It believes that everyone, deep inside, is the same, which means to most Americans that everyone, deep inside, is like them, and this, at times, is a problem. The United States is now and will be in the future the most important player on the team. It has to decide whether it needs to play mostly as a solo act and too often to lose, or whether it is willing to work together with others and more often to win. And if the United States loses, we all lose. As Canadians, we know how to live together as diverse peoples. We know how to live together in a diverse world. No other country in the next fifty years will have a greater impact on the world, good or bad, than the United States. There is no more important role for Canada to play in the world than to help make the impact of the United States constructive and good. Much of that will happen indirectly. In how Canada relates to the rest of the world, it will show the United States the way.

The referendums in Quebec in 1980 and 1995 forced all Canadians, not only Quebeckers, to think about Canada, to ask ourselves, What *is* Canada and why does Canada matter? Making the case for Canada, or for any country, is not as easy as it seems. When we try, when our words come out, they sound so trite and embarrassing even to our own ears, as if we're selling what we don't really believe we should have to sell. If Californians were to vote on the independence of California, how would Americans sell America? How would the English sell the Scots? How would the Flemish sell the Walloons? In 1995, Canada's politicians sold to Quebeckers the physical glories of the country—the Rocky Mountains, the prairies, the lakes and rivers and the boundless North—they belong to you too, Quebeckers were reminded. Why would you give them up? And . . . and, Canada's politicians continued, . . . and we all live pretty well here. What would happen to all of that if you left? And don't think that you would be able to keep all of the old that you want, and have all of the new as well. Canadians are going to take your rejection of Canada personally. They are going to take it as a rejection of themselves. Will you need a new currency of your own? What about your economy? More companies will leave the province. What about your share of the national debt? During the referendum campaign, the story of an independent Quebec seemed so complicated, so risky, so unknown.

That was the story pitched to Quebeckers—the Rockies and the fear of the unknown. To those outside Quebec, it was so frustrating. We are more than this. We know it; we feel it.

The story on the *indépendentiste* side was so simple and evocative. Finally, a country of our own. Finally, we can be what *we* want to be. Finally, *our* language, *our* thinking, *our* ways. Finally, *maîtres chez nous*.

The result: 50.58 per cent No to 49.42 per cent Yes. But even at that moment many Canadians outside Quebec believed that some day a fearful story wouldn't be enough. To win in the future, we need a bigger story of Canada to tell.

Quebec is so central to this new story of Canada. This story has emerged from the Canadian experience of our Aboriginal peoples, then of our French and English peoples living side by side with different languages, cultures, religions, and laws that forced us to deal with difference. We had to learn to accept and respect difference, to negotiate and compromise, to learn how to live with difference. And despite tensions that are never not there, and sensitivities that are never quite understood, we have learned—we know—this country can work. We have learned about language, and how a language majority doesn't think much about the importance of language, and how a language minority thinks about little else, and how, to that language minority, language is survival. Language is existence. We have learned that our difference and tension never go away—they have no final resolution—but that is what diversity and richness bring, and we have learned that we don't want them to go away, that we are smarter and more complex and more complicated and more interesting because of them. These are our national learnings, all of these learnings are inside us, inside Albertans and Nova Scotians, inside Ontarians and Manitobans, inside Quebeckers. And what is inside us is what needs to be inside all of us in a global world. This is Canada. This is Quebec.

If we understand the specialness of our own story, a next referendum in Quebec is less likely. If we understand the specialness of our own story, if there is a next referendum, there will be—finally—a big, compelling Canada story to tell.

—

As American venture capitalist and writer Guy Kawasaki has said, "Some things need to be believed to be seen." This story of Canada has been in us all along, hidden by history and circumstance, hidden by modesty, hidden by irony and self-deprecation, hidden by politics. But the world has changed, and Canada has changed. We need to believe this, to see this, to be what we are. It is not easy for anyone to give up what they are. We are good at being us; we know how to do it. We don't yet know how to be the more that is in us. We have always been a "yes, but . . ." country, willing to acknowledge what others say we are, then quick to smother that in perspective. It is time to be more "yes" and less "but." Every true story is part fact, part hopeful fiction; part what is, part what credibly can be; part "yes," part "but"; part reality, part aspirational tale. "America" is not a physical place. It is a place of the heart and of the imagination. If we believe the story of this Canada, and see it, what might "Canada" be? This country that is the most global country in a global world, and *knows* it, what would it do about—climate change, poverty, starvation, human rights? How will our political parties, how will the Liberals and Conservatives, how will the New Democrats, Bloc, and Green reflect this Canada? How will the political media reflect this Canada? How will our politics be confronted, challenged, and changed? How will Canadians react to all the possibilities and obligations of this new story? What will Canadians do? With so much in us, what further story will we write? Who knows? That is the exciting part. This is "Canada."

EPILOGUE

In earlier Olympic Games, summer and winter,
Canada had won many medals. Percy Williams in 1928
and Donovan Bailey in 1996 won the men's 100 metre
sprint. Several rowers, canoeists, and swimmers in
particular had won gold medals, a few of whose names
and those of many other Olympians still linger in our
memory years later: Barbara Ann Scott, Nancy Greene,
Barbara Wagner and Bob Paul, Jamie Salé and David
Pelletier, Gaétan Boucher, Alex Bauman, Marnie
McBean, Lennox Lewis, Marc Gagnon, and Catriona
Le May Doan. Canada had by far its best Olympic
Games in terms of total medals won in Los Angeles in
1984 with forty-four medals, of which ten were gold,
yet this had been an Olympics that all of the Eastern
Bloc countries, except China and Romania, including
Olympic powerhouses the Soviet Union and East

Germany, had boycotted. At Seoul, four years later, Canada returned to more traditional medal levels, winning ten, three of them gold. It seemed that as every new Olympic Games approached, Canadians knew that by skill and by law of averages somehow we would win some medals, though we had no idea who our medallists would be. That is, until Turin in 2006.

In Turin, Cindy Klassen, Clara Hughes, and Jennifer Heil all won gold medals, and so did the men's curlers and women's hockey team among others, twenty-four medals in all, seven of them gold, the third highest medal total of all the countries who participated, behind Germany and the United States. But more than that, in Turin we had lots of other athletes who came close to winning and who were young, and who had even better years ahead. And four years later, we had the Winter Games again, this time on our own home ground in Vancouver.

To set the ambitions for the Vancouver Games, a new sports agency was created in Canada, led by former athletes and with the spirit of athletes. This group was not interested in modest self-deprecation. We are better than we have ever been, it reasoned, and we are going to be so much better in the future, and anybody who is paying even the slightest attention knows this. It is time to say what we are and be what we are. It is time for Canada to "Own the Podium." The group chose this as its slogan. This was to be Canada's Olympic story.

It is easy for a national Olympic organization to talk about its athletes "doing their best" or achieving "personal bests." In the event of failure, such words can be finessed to sound almost like success. "Own the Podium" can't.

The host city of an Olympic Games buys the right to create athletic and other facilities, and the rest of the world largely pays for them through the sale of television rights, corporate sponsorships, and event tickets. In addition, a host city and a host country buys the opportunity for seventeen days (and for many more days leading up to the Games) to tell the story of itself that it wants billions of people to know. Because television rights are so expensive, rights holders can justify what they have spent only by filling the screens in their own home countries for most of those seventeen days with Olympic coverage, and there are not Olympic events going on all that time, and most of the events are in sports that most people don't know and never see except every four years. What a home audience sees— an audience that is nearly everywhere in the world— are hours and hours of remarkable, likeable triumphs, even likeable disasters, in front of thousands of excited, cheering, likeable people, all of this surrounded by even more hours and hours of genial "good news" hosts, not cynical news journalists, who offer the story around the Games, the warm, affectionate human nature stories that reflect, in this case, the people of Vancouver and the people of Canada.

Before the Games began, foreign journalists helped to set the scene for their audiences at home. Rick Reilly, a prominent American sports journalist formerly with *Sports Illustrated*, told Americans what they already knew about Canada so that they wouldn't need to look for more, managing to squeeze into a few hundred words one "moose," one "beaver," a "malamute," one "Gretz" and two "Wayne[s]," a "colder 'n a Newfie's arse," and several references to nice—"These people are nice. Preposterously nice. Aunt Bee in mukluks nice." The *New York Times'* media editor, Bruce Headlam, a Canadian, offered many of these same old references, even managing to connect a "beaver" with niceness, informing us that "Beaver will only chew off their testicles if you ask nicely." Before and during the Games, some television ads even in Canada offered the same predictable message. The spokesperson for President's Choice foods, Galen Weston Jr., great-grandson of parent-company founder George Weston, told Canadians of the role President's Choice played in feeding the Canadian alpine ski team. If that helped them to win races, he said, President's

Choice would take some credit. "But not too much," he continued. "After all [wry smile], we are Canadian."

The opening ceremonies were mystical and beautiful, respectful and proud, without any of the edge of "Own the Podium," which said about Canada to the world, "We are good." A malfunction of a hydraulic cauldron left Olympic gold medallist Catriona Le May Doan with a lighted torch to hold and nothing to light. Under other circumstances, this mishap might have been shrugged off, but it came only a few hours after a luge athlete from Georgia had lost control on a training run, crashed, and died. It also came only a few hours before warm weather caused a postponement of the men's downhill ski race. This postponement came only a few hours before a ninety-minute delay at the speed skating oval when the ice-surfacing machines didn't work. A few hours later, twenty thousand ticket holders were told they would get their money back but would lose their chance to watch snowboarding events because their place to stand had melted away. For Canadians, who had anticipated these Games for so long, who were so ready to be excited and proud, and who had yet no Canadian medals to focus them and distract them, this series of mishaps was embarrassing and unsettling. Perhaps we had it all wrong. Perhaps we weren't as good as we thought we were.

Before we had the chance to conclude this way again, others, most notably in the British press, concluded this way for us. An article in the *Guardian* stated, "Vancouver Games continue downhill slide from disaster to calamity," which, according to its subtitle, threatened to make these Games "the worst in Olympic history." The Canadian media, which had also been critical of the glitches, and which was just beginning to build toward its "Typically Canadian, eh?" lament, suddenly found itself in the unfamiliar position of instinctively offering defence against the media overreactions of others. As for Canadians, they knew only that they didn't want to believe what the Brits were saying. Their sense of propriety and proportion was offended. They knew, We may not be as good as we would like to be, but we aren't as bad as they say we are.

Then the situation got worse. At the end of the first week, as the United States, Germany, and Norway kept piling up the medals, it became clear that Canada would not "Own the Podium." Like any such phrase, "Own the Podium" had been intended more as a rallying cry than as a promise. We had won more medals in Turin than we had ever won before, and now this was our own home rink. Why not aspire? Why not dream? Why not reach for and find all that is in us? But at the end of that first week, it didn't feel that way. To many Canadians, and to many in the media, we had overreached. As host, we had got too carried away with ourselves. Who did we think we were? We had shown to the world and to ourselves a new arrogant face of Canada that we didn't recognize and didn't like. What is wrong with doing our best? What is wrong with being nice? It took the second week for us to find our own answers. In the second week, we began to win.

As all this national soul-baring was going on, Canadian athletes remained largely unaffected and un-impressed. They were focused on their task; more than that, they already knew their own answers. In all the years that they had been out of sight to the Canadian public, they had been working and competing, getting better and better. They had learned to deal with the good and the bad, they had put themselves up against the world. They had learned about the world, they had learned about themselves, they had learned how to win. They already knew what Canadians watching them at that moment should have known about themselves, and through them were now about to learn again.

What does nice have to do with winning? The person most associated with the phrase "Nice guys finish last" was baseball manager Leo Durocher, who won only one World Series in more than twenty-five seasons. Think of the best of the best, our greatest athletes and artists—Wayne Gretzky, Alice Munro, Bobby Orr, Terry Fox, Margaret Atwood, Guy Laliberté, Steve Nash, Joni Mitchell, and so on. Being nice has nothing to do with being the best or with being the worst, just as being nasty doesn't either. Being the best has to do with being so absorbed in what you're doing that you have no time for attitude. You have no time for yourself separate from what you're doing. What you are doing, you know, is more important than you are. And because you know this, no matter how good you are, no matter how good you become, you are never good enough. The great always fall short in their own minds; the great remain fiercely proud, yet humble. They know they are not as good as they seem to be. It is the almost-greats, those who might even have the talent of the greats but who are so preoccupied with themselves that they seek out every camera, they are the ones who strut. They are the ones who give winning a bad name.

On their television screens, Canadians saw a different image. First, there was Alexandre Bilodeau, with his parents and his brother, Frédéric, who has cerebral palsy, watching, anxious, hopeful, and finally exultant as Alexandre won Canada's first gold medal on Canadian soil. Then came Maëlle Ricker, Christine Nesbitt, and Jon Montgomery. In the second week, the gold medals came in a rush: Ashleigh McIvor; Tessa Virtue and Scott Moir in ice dance, who, after skating with each other for most of their lives, after growing up together, in front of our eyes somehow had matured *together* into this impossibly beautiful pair. Then Kaillie Humphries and Heather Moyse; the women's hockey team; Charles Hamelin; Jasey-Jay Anderson; then the men's speed skating and short track speed skating relay teams, and the men's curling team. There was also bronze-medallist Joannie Rochette, who by continuing to skate understood better than anyone that she couldn't allow the pain of not competing or not competing at her best to compound the pain of losing her mother. Then, finally, on television in front of 80 per cent of the entire population of Canada who watched at least part of the game, 80 per cent that has never come together for *anything* ever before, there was the men's hockey team, in overtime. For seventeen days, event after event, interview after interview, Canadians had been immersed in the faces of these athletes and in the faces of many others who did not win gold medals or win any medals at all. Strong faces; healthy faces; alive faces. Do you think any of them even for a moment didn't have in their minds to "Own the Podium"? Not a chance. And then there was that final winning face, in overtime, of Sidney Crosby. These were the faces of Canadians.

Of the eighty-two countries that participated, Canada finished third in total medals with twenty-six, behind the United States and Germany. Fourteen of these medals were gold, four more than any other country, and the most gold medals ever won by any country in any single Winter Olympic Games.

During the Olympics, the phrase "Own the Podium" had been a source of national debate and division. Since the Olympics, it has become part of our daily language. "Own the Podium" is now part of how we think and part of who we are. Sometimes you have to believe to see. In those seventeen days in Vancouver, Canada's athletes blew apart the last remnants of an old, crippling story. It wasn't their story, just as it's not the story of Canadian writers and musicians, scientists, and all kinds of other people in many, many fields. It's not what they have experienced in their lives. It is not their Canada.

These Olympic athletes won because winning was in them. They won because it is in us. In Vancouver, we discovered we are good. Now it is time for us to be important too.